M000276498

EIB Education
New King's House,
136-144 New Kings Road,
London, SW6 4LZ,
United Kingdom
www.eibeducation.com

Ordering Information: Quantity sales: special discounts are available on quantity purchases by schools, corporations, associations, and others. For details, contact the publisher at the address above.

First published in the United Kingdom in 2019
Printed and bound in the United Kingdom
ISBN: 978-1-83853-038-9

Director
Timothy Hoffmann

Editor-at-Large
Bella Southworth-Simons

Editor
Sam Romeo

The IB Guide

by EIB Education

Contents

1.
Intro

1. Introduction

1.1 Who we are

EIB Education are a passionate team of former IB students, dedicated to ensuring every student, parent, and IB educator has access to all the IB information they need to get the most out of this incredible educational model. We are unabashed in our love of the IB, but appreciate some of its terminology and peculiarities can be difficult to understand at first, and so we spend our working lives speaking with IB students, graduates, tutors, teachers, and parents, to provide guidance no matter where you are in your IB journey. Our core contributing team for this guide has comprised of:

Tim

Tim is the Director of EIB Education, and firmly of the belief that the International Baccalaureate's educational ethos and structure makes it the foremost school-leaving qualification worldwide. Tim completed the IB at Antwerp International School in 2005 obtaining 44 points and went on to obtain an MEng from St Edmund Hall, Oxford University, in 2009. He has been tutoring IBDP & MYP candidates since 2006, and founded EIB in 2010.

Charlotte

Charlotte is the Head of Operations for EIB Switzerland. She attended *La Châtaigneraie* where she passed her IGCSEs and IBDP with flying colours, progressing to a BSc Hons Biochemistry and Masters in Molecular Biology and Pathology of Viruses from Imperial College London. Alongside her work with EIB, Charlotte is also studying Graduate Medicine at the highly prestigious St. George's, London.

Laura

As Client & Education Manager in Switzerland, Laura is responsible for responding to client enquiries and ensuring that students are paired with the very best tutors. Laura studied her IGCSEs and the IBDP in Geneva, where she grew up, and score 45 points before studying Geography at the University of Cambridge. For several years she tutored Geography, French Literature, and Biology.

Wei Hao

Wei Hao is the Director of EIB in Singapore. Following his completion of his GCSEs at the British School in the Netherlands, and his IB in UWC S.E. Asia, he went on to attain First Class honours in his MChem Chemistry at the University of Oxford. Wei Hao then completed his DPhil in Physical and Theoretical Chemistry, also at Oxford.

Bella

Bella is our Head of Tutoring & Consulting and an experienced tutor and university application consultant. She completed her International Baccalaureate studies in Cornwall before graduating from King's College, London in 2014, with a BA English Language and Literature, followed in 2015 by her MA Modern Culture & Theory.

Ebba

Ebba is EIB's Head of Courses and Events. A truly international IB student, Ebba completed her pre-university studies across multiple countries and continents, before completing both her BA Politics and MA Diplomacy at a top university in the UK.

Abby

Abby is a Client and Operations Manager for EIB. After completing the International Baccalaureate DP in Leicester, Abby studied Natural Sciences at the University of Cambridge, followed by an MSc, also at Cambridge, in the History and Philosophy of Science.

We have also had the fortune to be able to draw on the IB experiences of others, who we could not have completed this IB Guide without, including but not limited to other EIB team members, our tutoring team, and our students. The full list of contributors is listed in the appendix.

1.2 Who this guide is for

We have tried to make the IB Guide accessible to everyone, whether you are totally new to the world of the IB or a Coordinator looking for study tips for your students.

1.3 What this guide includes

Information on the IB
- Advice from IB graduates
- Useful IB resources section
- Detailed guidance on the EE, TOK, and CAS
- Organisation and revision tips
- UK university application advice
- Exam checklist
… *and much, much more!*

1.4 Who is the *IB Guide* for?

Packed full of information about every aspect of the International Baccalaureate, written by IB educators with years of experience, it's a treasure trove for anybody needs to know anything IB-related, including:

- **Students** – With revision tips, subject-specific and IA guidance, and advice on managing stress and your time, there's wealth of advice for students here.
- **Parents** – From advice on school-selection, unpicking the IB's various acronyms, and university applications, there's plenty to help parents get to grips with the IB syllabus to support their children.
- **Educators** – An introduction to every aspect of the IB, the *IB Guide* is a great introduction to recently accredited IB schools, who are going through authorisation.

1.5 When to use the *IB Guide*

Students:
We hope this will not be something you read once and consign to the dustiest corner of your bookshelf! Instead, we hope to have insights relevant to all stages of your IB journey, from selecting your IB subjects to life after the IB, with plenty of key information targeting every point in an IB student's life- managing IA deadlines, deciding on an Extended Essay topic, how on earth to revise for six subjects at once, to name but a few.

Parents
An IB education is a wonderful gift, and can open doors for your children forever, but there's no getting away from the fact that the IBO exists in its own world, much as does any all-encompassing education system. Use this guide to become *au fait* with the IB before your child, or children, embark on their IB adventure, but be sure to check back throughout the years to remind yourself of any key terminology and to stay on top of their upcoming deadlines.

IB Educators
Whether you are a seasoned IB educator, or a teacher moving to the IB system for the first time, we hope you are as enthusiastic about IB teaching methods and the IB programmes as we are! We hope to have created an IB Guide you can dip in and out of throughout your time as an IB Educator, with sections you can pass through to your students and others which you may find informative yourself. If you feel there are further IB queries we have not tackled in this edition of the IB Guide, please do let us know, and we will be sure to address these in later revisions.

2.
About
the IB

2. About the IB

2.1 What is the IBO?

The International Baccalaureate Organisation (IBO) is an international educational organisation which offers students a holistic and global education through successive IB programmes aimed at students around the world from the age of 3 to 19. The most widely known and studied programme internationally is the IBDP or the 'International Baccalaureate Diploma Programme'. Initially founded in Geneva in 1968, the IBO now offers IB programmes in over 130 countries around the world.

2.2 What are the IB Programmes?

Diploma Programme

The IBDP (International Baccalaureate Diploma Programme) is a post-secondary, pre-university education programme, taken by students around the world between the ages of 16 and 18 or 19. It is an equivalent qualification to the UK's A-levels, the US's AP exams, and the Scottish Highers System, and was the first programme developed and offered by the IB. The Diploma Programme is internationally well-regarded, and has been the pathway for thousands of students entry into universities and employment around the world.

The IB also provide curricula for younger students: the PYP, or Primary Years Programme, embodies the IB's international, multidisciplinary approach to learning for 3-12 year olds. The MYP (Middle Years Programme) offers students aged 11-16 the opportunity to learn in an ongoing environment which fosters curiosity and breadth of learning.

Career-Related Programme:

The IBO run two programmes for 16-18 or 19-year-olds, the better-known and older Diploma Programme, which much of this guide is focused on, and the newer Career-related Programme. The Career-related Programme gives students the opportunity to focus their advanced learning on skills relevant to employment, taking on fewer IB subjects, while also gaining practical skills and experience to equip students for apprenticeships, careers, or additional education.

Similar to the DP, the CP has a 'core', comprised of personal & professional skills, service learning, language development, and a reflective project. Students then take a minimum of two Diploma Programme courses; each school selects the subjects is makes available to CP students, but these can be drawn from any subject group as offered in the DP. In addition to the core and the DP courses, Career-related Programme students must also complete their career-related study, as awarded by their career-related study provider.

Students looking to prepare themselves for entering the workforce rather than focusing solely on academic study are advised to consider the Career-related Programme, which is now offered by over 140 schools across 23 countries. While the content of the DP courses is the same whether taken by a Diploma or Career-related Programme student, the additional focus on career-related skills provide CP students with the opportunity to target their academic learning towards their future careers aim(s) and to prepare to make meaningful advances early in their employed life.

While the CP is recognised by some universities, it does not have the near-universal recognition of the Diploma Programme, and so for students certain they are aiming for university, the DP might be a better choice of programme. However, for students with a good understanding of their academic area(s) of interest and keen to begin their career as promptly as possible but with a strong education behind them, the CP may be an ideal fit.

At EIB, we are most experienced at providing support in all aspects of the Diploma Programme, and so much of the following information is DP-focused, but we are always happy to receive queries on the MYP, PYP, and CP, and if we do not have the answers to hand, rest assured we will find them for you!

Inquirers
Knowledgeable
Thinkers
Commucators
Principled
Open-Minded
Caring
Risk-Takers
Balanced
Reflective

IB Learner Profile

2.3 How is the DP organised?

An IBDP student normally takes 6 academic subjects, as well as completing an independently researched Extended Essay, participating in Theory of Knowledge, and carrying out multiple and varied projects to fulfil their Creativity, Activity, and Service requirements. Only upon successful completion of all these components is an IB graduate awarded the full IB Diploma.

Subject requirements

All IBDP students take six academic subjects, fulfilling specific criteria to ensure a well-rounded pattern of subjects, as well as compulsory CAS, TOK, and the EE. Completion of all components of the IBDP is necessary for a student to be awarded the Diploma, although students can receive subject certificates in each subject they pass, should they fail to receive the full Diploma. For most universities with academic entrance requirements, however, the full Diploma is required.

Groups

Students must take a subject which falls into each of Groups 1-5, listed and explained below. Students can choose to not take a Group 6 subject (Arts), and can instead take another Group 1-4 subject to bring their total subjects to the compulsory 6. Please see Appendix 1 for the full list of subjects currently offered worldwide for each group.

Group 1: Studies in Language and Literature

This is usually the student's first language, and will require fluency in the language chosen. Students will tackle literary texts in this language, and all examinations and internally assessed work in this subject will be in the chosen language. Students who are able to can opt to take two languages at this level, and will be awarded a bilingual Diploma upon successful completion of both subjects.

Group 2: Language Acquisition

Students can choose to take a language without prior study (*ab initio*), or can build on pre-existing knowledge of a language. This must not be the student's first language, as the course aims to develop language-learning ability, as well as a deeper understanding of another culture.

Group 3: Individuals & Societies

Students choose from a range of Humanities subjects, including but not limited to, History, Geography, Economics, and Business Management. This Group provides students with the opportunity to explore societal, political, economic, and environmental structures and their impact globally.

Group 4: Sciences

Any of the traditional Science subjects can be chosen here, as well as Environmental Systems & Societies (ESS), which can be taken as either a Group 3 or 4 subject, and Computer Science, Design Technology, and Sports Science. This Group encourages students to understand the global application of scientific solutions, as well as the theory and context of their chosen Science, which is further challenged by a compulsory group project, named the Group 4 project.

Group 5: Maths

Students must take a level of Mathematics, but can choose from a wider range than usual; Mathematics SL and HL are offered, as for most subjects, but students can also choose Mathematical Studies, only offered as an SL subject, or Further Mathematics, which is only offered as an HL subject. Most students who opt to take Further Maths will also take Maths HL, as this is a requirement of almost every school which offers this elective subject. Please note that the IBO are overhauling Maths as part of the Diploma from 2019, for first examinations in 2021, offering two different Maths courses, both available at HL and SL. One will focus on Pure Maths, while the other will centre on Applied Mathematics, resulting, the IBO hope, in Maths courses which provide students with critical thinking skills as well as a level of Maths engagement appropriate to the student's interest and ability in this area. Further Maths will no longer be taught on the IB, with the IBO suggesting students with a particular interest in Mathematics carry out their Extended Essay in this are to further their IB Maths engagement. *N.B. The IBO are rolling out significant changes to Group 5 subjects from 2018/19, see 2.6.3b.*

Group 6: Arts

The Arts choices include Visual Arts, Drama, Film, and Music, each of which focus on creatively exploring self-expression in a global context, and developing their own unique critical practice. A student may opt not to take a Group 6 subject, and

instead take a further subject in a language (Groups 1 & 2), a social science (Group 3), or a science (Group 4).

Higher Level / Standard Level (HL/SL)

Each of the DP subjects carry a subject 'level', and a Diploma student must take at least 3 subjects at Higher Level (HL), and no more than three at Standard Level (SL). Some students choose to take an additional HL subject, but it is advised to discuss this well in advance with your school or education provider. As a rough indication of the difficulty of each level, the IB advises approximately 240 hours of teaching time for HLs and 160 for SLs, and the difference between HL and SL in each subject varies, so it is best to discover what 'extras' you are able to study by opting for HL in each of your subjects. Some subjects (ESS, Maths Studies, Further Maths) are only available at one level, and so it is vital that this is taken into consideration when making final subject selections.

Points, grading, assessment

Diploma subjects are graded 1-7, with 7 being the top, A* equivalent, grade. On average, about 7% of IB students around the world achieve a grade 7, although this varies from subject to subject, with more students attaining a 7 in language acquisition than any other subject group. The mean grade for any subject across the Diploma is 4.81. This gives a total possible score of 42 from 6 academic subjects, and an additional 3 bonus points are available for the 'core' (TOK & EE, *see* 3.4); the top possible IB score is therefore 45. In May 2017, 278 of almost 160,000 candidates achieved 45 points, while the global average points score was 29.87[1]- meaning a tiny proportion of students achieve or come close to the full 45 points every year.

The DP runs for two academic years, with final exams taking place at the end of the 2nd year ("IBDP2"). The Diploma is assessed in a linear, not modular, manner, and all external (generally exam-based) assessment therefore takes place at the end

---

of the 2 years. There are two exam 'seasons', to reflect the two hemispheres' academic years; students will variously sit their final exams in May or November. For Northern hemisphere/May season candidates, their IBDP1 year will begin in August or September, and they will take exams in the May two years after: for instance, students who began their IB studies in August or September 2017 will take their exams in May 2019. For Southern hemisphere / November season candidates, the commencing month is January or February, and exams are in the following November.

Each Group has its own ways of assessing students, and Higher / Standard Level discrepancies; we recommend viewing the specific 'subject brief' for each of your preferred subjects before making a final decision on which to take. These are accessible at all times through the IBO website, but please do ensure you have the most recent subject briefs when using these to make your decision, as assessment methods can change from one curriculum review to another.

For Group 1, students at both HL & SL sit during the final exam session an examination paper assessing their ability to analyse unseen text, as well as an examination paper on texts they have studied (this varies for *Literature & Performance*, but two external exams are undertaken in this course also). All students also submit a number (varied across specific subjects & level) of written tasks (akin to coursework) and undertake several oral assessments, prior to the final exam session.

For Group 2, students at HL, SL, and *ab initio* level, of both modern & classic languages, undertake two examination papers, the first of which is focused on text handling and translation, and the second of which is focused on producing writing in the target language. As in Group 1, there are also several written tasks and oral components, one of each of which is submitted for assessment as part of the final grade.

For Group 3, students at SL follow the format of two final exam papers, and internally assessed written

work. For many HL students, however, Group 3 brings a third examination paper, pushing the student to engage further with the subject. Additionally, for many Group 3 subjects, the internally assessed work takes the form of several pieces of work, forming a portfolio, or project.

For Group 4, there is a larger variance across subjects regarding the exact nature of assessment. For the 'core' sciences of Biology, Chemistry, and Physics, there are 3 exam paper and internally assessed practicals/investigations, at both SL & HL. For all other Group 4 subjects, SL students undertake 2 exams, and many HL students undertake 3, each carrying out a personal project or investigation too. In addition, there is the Group 4 project, which contributes to the personal engagement marks of each student's overall Internal Assessment (IA) score. The Group 4 Project is a chance to work collaboratively with your fellow students across the sciences, so it is worth getting stuck into!

Students of the core Group 5 subjects will sit 2 or 3 exam papers, depending on the level of study, and complete a Maths 'exploration', or 'project' for Studies students, which constitutes the internally assessed component of the course. Students of Further Mathematics sit two external papers and do not complete any internally assessed work.

For those who opt to take a Group 6 subject, there is a significant disparity in the proportion of work which is exam-based, as many of the Group 6 subjects are assessed on the student's development over time and their creative output. This does not mean the work is not externally assessed, but Group 6 subjects will have a different timetable of assessment to the majority of other IB subjects- the key exception is Music, which has an exam in the same session as all other subjects. Many Group 6 students put a significant amount of personal time into developing their artistic practice, and so a method of continual assessment is valued in these areas in order to ensure the student is reaching their aims at each key stage of the IB.

For most subjects, the largest proportion of a student's final grade will come from their final exams, but internally assessed work counts for 15-30% of each subject's final grade, providing a great confidence boost when sitting the finals, as students know they have made headway towards their desired grade before even beginning their exam.

Bilingual Diploma

What is the IB Bilingual Diploma?

The IB Bilingual Diploma is a version of the IB Diploma. It is awarded to candidates who demonstrate language proficiency in two different languages.

How can I obtain the Bilingual Diploma?

There are two different ways to obtain a Bilingual Diploma:
Completion of two languages from group 1 (i.e. two language A subjects) scoring a 3 or higher in both.
or:
Completion of one of the subjects from group 3 (*Individuals and Societies*) or group 4 (*Experimental Sciences*) in a language that is not the same as your group 1 language, **scoring** a 3 or higher in both the group 1 language and the subject from group 3 or 4.

What are the advantages of obtaining a Bilingual Diploma?

Universities may require non-native students evidence of proficiency in the language of instruction, so the Diploma could be used as proof of language proficiency. There are also the general benefits of attaining proficiency in more than one language. Bilingualism may be an advantage in employment where languages are required. Additionally, students will have a wider choice of universities to attend in both languages.

What are the differences between the IB Diploma and the Bilingual Diploma?

The Bilingual Diploma requires you to either take two language A subjects from group 1 or do either a group 3 or group 4 subject in a language different to your group 1 language.

The *"regular"* IB Diploma only requires you to take a second language from group 2, and your other subjects will be in your group 1 language.

Do universities regard the Bilingual Diploma differently to the normal Diploma?

Universities do not usually regard the Bilingual and IB Diplomas differently, though some universities may accept the Bilingual Diploma as proof of language proficiency for non-native candidates. However, as universities aim to supply the market with bilingual graduates, demonstrating bilingualism may serve as an advantage in application procedures.

What are the general benefits of a bilingual education?

Bilingual individuals have an advantage in the current competitive job market, as employers see several advantages in hiring bilingual employees. It has been argued that bilingual people have superior linguistic cognitive skills and are more multicultural, which is key in a globalised society. It can also help you to develop an insightful understanding of two different cultures.

Irregular Diploma

What is an irregular diploma?

A student will obtain an irregular diploma if they choose to study three subjects from the same subject group and none from two groups: arts and another group of their choice. Choosing two subjects from the same subject group and none from arts is still a regular diploma and will have no complications regarding the irregular diploma.

When will I need an irregular diploma?

A student may need or may choose to pursue an irregular diploma if the university course they wish to apply to requires three subjects that belong to the same subject group in IB. This usually occurs with medical schools in some countries such as Sweden and India which require students to take all three science subjects in order to apply.

Do I automatically get an irregular diploma by simply choosing three subjects?

To have a valid irregular diploma, the student – in collaboration with their school – must show proof of why their subject choices are necessary for their further education. The IBO may then grant special permission for the student to continue with three subjects from the same subject group.

Can I apply for an irregular diploma if I have a strong interest in a subject group?

A student may apply for an irregular diploma, but the IBO may choose to not grant special permission for it if they consider an irregular diploma is not necessary for the student's further education.

How hard is the irregular diploma?

The difficulty of the irregular diploma highly depends on the student's subject choices and higher level choices, as well as how confident they feel in them and how much they enjoy their subjects. Having an irregular diploma, such as taking three science subjects, does not necessarily mean it will be more difficult than regular diplomas.

Would having an irregular diploma look bad on admissions?

University admissions may prefer an irregular diploma if the student has taken subjects which will be useful or are necessary for enrolment in the particular university course. Similarly, they may be unsatisfied with a student's irregular diploma if it lacks subjects which the university considers important for the student to start their further education in the course they choose. Simply having an irregular diploma will not necessarily benefit or hinder a student's application.

Theory of Knowledge (TOK)

One of the IB's additional compulsory aspects is TOK (Theory of Knowledge). This, combined with the EE, constitutes the additional 3 bonus points that students may accrue. To fail both TOK & the EE is a failing condition of the Diploma, no matter the student's academic attainment. Theory of Knowledge is an interdisciplinary study in critical thinking and encourages discussion of the extent &

limits of knowledge through an epistemological framework.

TOK focuses around examining Knowledge Questions through *Areas of Knowledge*, and *Ways of Knowing*.

Mathematics
Natural Sciences
Human Sciences
History
The Arts
Ethics
Religious Knowledge
Indigenous Knowledge

Areas of Knowledge

TOK is assessed through two pieces of work produced by each student: an in-class presentation, and an essay.
The essay, two-thirds of the TOK grade, is a 1200-1600 word response to one of six set questions, which change each year. Students are assessed on their ability to understand knowledge questions, and on the quality of their analysis, using real-life examples to illustrate pertinent explorations of the question.

In the presentation, which makes up the last third of the TOK grade, students are assessed on how well they show that TOK concepts have real-world applications. Here, students present either individually or as part of a group on a topic of their choice, and discuss a knowledge question which arises from a real-life event. Perspective and balance are key to a top TOK presentation, as well as personal engagement and use of TOK-specific terminology.

Language
Sense perception
Emotion
Reason
Imagination
Faith
Intuition
Memory

Ways of Knowing

Extended Essay (EE)

The second compulsory aspect of the Diploma which contributes to the potential 3 bonus points is the Extended Essay, a 4,000 word study in a subject and specific area of the student's choice. Each IB school typically has its own policy regarding Extended Essays and students are broadly encouraged to write their EE in a subject area that they already study as part of their Diploma studies, in a subject they pursue at Higher Level, and on a topic which bears relevance to their university programme of choice. The World Studies EE option, however, represents an interdisciplinary option which is not a stand-alone Diploma subject but which moves between two IBDP disciplines. Students interested in completing a World Studies EE must focus on an issue of global significance, demonstrating international-mindedness and global consciousness. It is advisable to have a clear idea of the area in question before committing to a World Studies EE, as the student must be supervised by a teacher at their IB World School, preferably with some experience of academia in this area. The Extended Essay is externally marked, but each student is closely supervised by a subject teacher, who also conducts the *viva voce* - a concluding interview once the EE has been completed. The Extended Essay is a significant piece of scholarship, and many IB students find it enormously rewarding. For many of the large proportion of IB students who go on to further study, the Extended Essay constitutes their first 'university-level' piece of academic work, and students often return to themes explored in their EE throughout their later studies.

Creativity, Activity, Service (CAS)

The final compulsory element of the IBDP does not contribute to the final IB Diploma score, but must be completed in order to attain the full Diploma. CAS (Creativity, Activity, Service) requires students to undertake projects demonstrating Creativity, Activity, and Service in various forms throughout the 2 years of the IBDP, encouraging well-rounded and community-aware students. Students must demonstrate they have met each of seven learning objectives through the programme, and many schools encourage students to begin and document one project or experience in each area per month through the Diploma. Students must also complete a CAS project, which involves working with others to demonstrate perseverance and commitment as well as planning and great team-work. Students are expected to "think global, act local", particularly with regards to the Service aspect of their CAS projects, as the IB encourages students to be aware of their place in their immediate community as well as a globally connected community.

The IB CAS requirement is a unique opportunity to receive credit for your interests outside of school , and this focus on developing students outside of the classroom as well as within is yet another reason that IB graduates are so well regarded by universities and employers.

Common examples for Creativity can include musical performance, acting, dancing, singing, and even cooking something new! For Activity, all sports, training, and sporting events can count, whether this is a solo or group activity, as long as they promote physical activity to benefit your health and you can clearly link your development to one of the CAS objectives. Finally, Service: volunteering of all kinds, from working in a charity shop to giving your time to mentor younger students, is accepted by the IB. The service aspect of CAS is something many IB graduates look back on with fondness, as it encourages students to think and act selflessly, even if for only an hour or two a week.

2.4 How is the IB regarded?

The IBDP is internationally regarded as an excellent and highly challenging qualification, and is internationally accepted by all top universities for undergraduate study. As such, it is easy for an IBDP student to apply through domestic university channels, as many universities have conversions from domestic systems to the IB - for example, A-level entry requirements to IBDP points. Please see below for a selection of university entry requirements for 2018 entry BSc Mathematics at a range of UK universities in IB points and their A-level equivalents as a beginning point of comparison:

- Cambridge: A*A*A + STEP[2]; 40-42 points (HLs of 776) + STEP
- Durham: A*A*A; 38 (HL subject requirements apply)
- York: AAA; 36 including 6 in HL Mathematics
- KCL: AAA (subject requirements); 35 including Core (HLs of 666)
- Brunel: AAB (A in Mathematics); 34 (HLs of 665, including Mathematics)

From these, it is clear to see that universities across the UK vary in their conversions between IBDP points and their UK equivalent, but also that all are

open to IBDP graduates. Please see the tariff provided by the central application body for UK universities (UCAS) for further details on their standardised conversion from IB Diploma scores to UCAS points, but do not forget to check the individual requirements for each of the universities you are considering applying to before making your application.

 Resources
eibeducation.com/resources
We have hundreds of IB resources to help you as you complete the IB, like our IB Requirements Matrix and our UCAS Calculator. You can get them all on our website.

The IBDP is also well-regarded in the US, with universities broadly equating it to the AP programme of study. The IB also has enormous prestige in universities around the world, including but not limited to, in Canada, mainland Europe, Singapore, China, and Australia. In some cases, IB studies can be counted towards the early stages of a university degree. The IB regularly publishes updated information on the Diploma and its level of recognition by universities around the world, so do be sure to check the IB website to see if they have created a factsheet for your preferred country of choice for university study.

In general, "higher education institutions around the world admit students based on their IB credentials", with research showing that IB graduates are significantly more likely to attend a selective or highly selective college in the US, more than twice as likely to attend a top 20 university in the UK, and that globally IB graduates adjust more easily to university studies than graduates of other equivalent programmes.[3]

[2] STEP, or Sixth Term Examination Paper Mathematics is "a well-established mathematics examination designed to test candidates on questions that are similar in style to undergraduate mathematics", Cambridge Assessment Admissions Testing, http://www.admissionstesting.org/for-test-takers/step/about-step/

[3] All from https://www.ibo.org/university-admission/recognition-of-the-ib-diploma-by-countries-and-universities/ib-diploma-compared-with-other-national-exams/

IB Graduate Skills

Many universities and employers value IBDP graduates. This is for several reasons, but most frequently we find the rigorous academic standards of the IB, the diversity of an IBDP education, and the consistency of grades awarded are extolled again and again. Further, the independent study required to excel in the IBDP ensures that IB students are experienced at time management and self-motivation.

The IB have a 'learner profile' for their Diploma Programme students, available online, which brings into one place each of the values the IB aims to develop in the DP students, under the umbrella of 'international-mindedness', the IB's overarching value. We have created our own version of this below, but encourage you also to look at the IB's graphic, to better understand their vision of international education and the characteristics fostered and developed by an IB education.

2.5 UK IB Schools

The IBO keep lists of all IB World Schools, arranged by country and which IB programme(s) they offer. At EIBm we try to keep up to speed on any changes to UK IB schools, and aim to have the most up-to-date UK school lists on our website, with associated profiles for some of the most popular Swiss, Singaporean, and Global IB schools also accessible. We are working to add profiles for an increasing number of countries, so if yours is not featured, please contact us to request this information.

UK IB schools are located across the nation, with clusters around major cities, and all four IB programmes are offered somewhere in the UK! Whilst A-levels are still the UK's most common pre-university qualification, UK universities widely recognise and value the IB, and do not hesitate to make offers to students of the programme.

Recent winners of the IB School of the Year[4] include Windermere (Lake District), Dartford Grammar (Dartford), King's College School (London), King Edward's School (Birmingham), Tonbridge Grammar (Kent) and the Stephen Perse Foundation (Cambridge), showing the wide spread of excellent IB teaching across the UK. The world average score in May 2017 (most recent May data available at time of press) for Diploma students was 29.87, and the UK's average in 2017 was 34.82, with 60 UK-based students achieving a perfect score of 45.[5] This further serves to show the enthusiasm with which UK schools, and most importantly, students, have taken to the IB.

 IB Schools
eibeducation.com/schools

We keep an up-to-date list of all the IB schools in the UK, Switzerland, and Singapore, with information on fees, programmes, and standard on the EIB Education website!

The MYP and UK schools

The Middle Years Programme, or MYP, is not taught in a large number of UK schools, particularly in comparison to the Diploma Programme- currently the IBO list only 14 schools offering the MYP, sat alongside 115 schools whose students can sit the Diploma. This may be for any number of reasons, including the UK education sector's strong tradition of splitting pre- and post-16 qualifications and offering these in differing institutions, or the ubiquity of the GCSE or IGCSE courses. However, as the final year of the MYP can now be assessed through optional externally moderated exams, MYP students are increasingly awarded certification in the same sense as (I)GCSE students, and so there may be a sharp increase over coming years in the number of UK schools offering the Middle Years Programme through to sixteen. The MYP's final exams are 'eAssessments', which are carried out on computers, and which aim to test student's processes and course understanding above memorisation or rote learning.

[4] Sunday Times IB School of the Year.
https://www.thetimes.co.uk/article/good-for-jagger-and-you-qs2x0dbh5v

[5] https://www.schoolhousemagazine.co.uk/news/ib-results-2017/

In this sense, the IB remain at the cutting edge of educational change, and this format may become more widespread over years to come. For more about MYP e-assessments, *see 4.2.*

2.6 IB Advice

In this section, we have compiled advice from our office team of IB graduates and some of our most trusted tutors, giving you a unique insight into the IB from those who loved our IB years so much we just couldn't let them go! Each and every member of our contributing team looks back on their IB years with fondness, but could perhaps have stood to listen to some of the following guidance to make the two years progress as smoothly as possible.

2.6.1 Why the IB - and why not?

The IB Diploma Programme is known as an academically rigorous, well-rounded, and internationally-minded programme, where students have to learn quickly to work independently and manage their time well. For some students, the prospect of balancing six subjects during the time they will also be applying to university and making major life decisions is thrilling, and for others, less so. While many students will enjoy the IBDP, and successfully navigate its path, there are some key considerations to think of before throwing yourself in- or out!

One common difficulty for prospective students is the inability to take three Science subjects- this can be a deciding factor for some students considering Medicine, for instance, but at the same time each year many IB students successfully gain places on some of the world's most competitive Medical programmes. *See 2.3* for information on the 'irregular diploma', available to some IB students with specific university requirements in this area.

Further, some students worry that taking six subjects can lead to a lack of depth in some areas, such as in your Standard Level subjects. Any student worried about this may consider reading through the syllabus or past exam papers across a range of qualifications, to make their own judgement on the breadth and depth of each subject in comparison to, for instance, their local or national curriculum equivalent.

Finally, for some students the idea of continuing Maths is a difficult one. The IB have acknowledged students engage with Maths in a variety of ways, and students have the greatest choice in the level of Maths they undertake, to try to make every IB student comfortable at the level they have chosen to study.

Key strengths of the programme include the breadth of study and the interdisciplinary approach to subjects; students are encouraged to learn and live as citizens of the world, rather than approaching their studies in a vacuum, and so each member of the IB community, while spread globally, carry the same ethos and approach to a connected world. A focus on developing critically-minded students in all areas means employers and universities are confident in an IB graduate's transferable skills, and a focus on language learning through an understanding of culture makes for considerate, internationally-minded, and independent students and global citizens. We recommend doing your own research, however, as here at EIB we love the IB and are undoubtedly biased in its favour!

2.6.2 Subject selection

Many students find it difficult to decide which subjects they should opt for on the Diploma Programme, and which to take at Higher and Standard Level. Honestly, there are no right or wrong answers to this question. Every student is different - you will have different interests, different aims, a different outlook on life, and you will most definitely have different strengths and weaknesses – and balancing these variables is extremely important. One of the key strengths and aims of the IBDP is to offer each student breadth and depth, a holistic education that will allow you to dip your toes into many different fields. The benefit of this to you is to allow you to spread your wings, while specialising in a few key fields. You need to start by asking yourself two key questions:

Firstly, what are your aims? You need to carefully consider what you might want to achieve at the end of your Diploma. For example, do you want to go to university? If so, are you aiming for universities of the standard of Oxford and Cambridge, or would you like to attend a college in London, somewhere else in Europe, or are you looking to study in the American system or indeed elsewhere? The importance of setting these goals is to ensure you have something to aim towards, and understand the amount of work you must put in to achieve this aim.

Secondly, what are your strengths and weaknesses? Think about your current studies- what subjects are you excelling in, and what are you struggling in? You may excel in the sciences and maths while your best friend triples your grades in the humanities and the arts. Studying what you enjoy and getting a sense of accomplishment from is important, and it will help you achieve more when it comes to taking exams. Naturally, as a prospective IB student it is likely that you have a range of interests, some of which may clash with one another when considering further study. Be sure to take your time considering your interests and strengths so that you are fully confident in your final decision.

HLs vs SLs

Let's start by assuming you've already picked your six IB subject- a difficult decision, but now you're ready to begin studying, right?

Unfortunately, the answer is no, because you still have to choose between Higher Level (HL) and Standard Level (SL) subjects. This is pretty important, as it will impact how much and what you study, your scores, and even if you'll be in the same class as your crush (unrelated to the IB but often a big factor nonetheless). So, what do you do?

As the names suggest, HLs are more advanced – they cover more material and are harder. Usually, students take 3 HLs and 3 SLs, though everyone's heard of that one student at that one school who took 4 HLs and 2 SLs, or even 5 HLs and 1 SL (although note that this would not allow you to attain

the Diploma if you maintained these all the way through the two years to final exams, as a minimum of 2 subjects must be taken at SL!). You can take 4 HLs if you want to and your school are happy for you to do so, but for most students and their university ambitions it is not advisable as there is no real need to do it in order to be able to submit competitive applications. But hey, if you want the challenge of having more HLs than SLs and feel capable of doing it, then go for it. Just don't complain if you can't go out on Friday night!

So, the issue here is: which subjects should you choose as HL and which as SL? Here are five things to consider when making the ultimate HL/SL decision.

Your Strengths and Weaknesses

Don't call me Captain Obvious yet. If you know you struggle with a subject, stick to the SL version. SL subjects are generally slightly easier and cover way less material than their HL versions. Conversely, you may wish to dedicate more time to your strengths – you will be more likely to get a 7 in a subject you are good at, even if it is HL. Not only you will enjoy your course more, you will feel less frustrated and more successful if you see yourself powering through the IB, which is great for your confidence and mental health – and who doesn't love that?

Time & Workload

HL subjects cover more topics than their SL counterparts, so you will spend more time studying these. Also, your teacher will go at a faster pace, so it can be stressful at times. For some subjects, like English Literature, the difference is that you'd have to read more novels and poetry for HL. For others, like Business & Management, the HL topics are supposedly more advanced than the core ones. You should look at the differences between HL and SL in each subject and decide if you are willing to do the extra work. Try to do the ones that you will enjoy the most – or cause you the least suffering.

University Course Requirements

Many universities, especially top ones, will have their own requirements for the course you want to do. Make sure you check your course at each of the universities you want to apply to; you might find that you must have a specific HL in order to apply. Even if there are no requirements, consider which subjects are better suited to prepare you for your degree. If you want to study Biochemistry at university, why would you do Chemistry SL and Art HL, for instance? You want to prepare yourself with the right subjects and let universities know you are prepared for their degree.

If you don't know what you want to study at university, or if you want to go to university at all, don't worry; you have time to find out (but start thinking about it, this isn't something you can *wing* the day before the deadline!).

IB Scores

This one links to the previous point. You can't get into university without your IB scores, and all universities have a minimum score for applying. You want to get as close to 45 points as possible while doing useful subjects for your university degree. I'm not supposed to say this, but in some subjects, it is easier to get a 7 than in others. So, for example, don't take Math HL just to show off if you don't need it for your university applications. I mean, would you rather get a 4 in Math HL and 33 points overall, or a 6 in Math SL and 35 overall? For some applications, a 2-point difference can be crucial. Of course, if you want an extra challenge and to take harder subjects at HL because you can handle it, then you should go for it. Just keep in mind the importance of IB scores in meeting university offers.

Weight of IAs and Exam Papers

This tip is a cheeky one, but a common way to help you decide your HLs. Your IA will be worth a different percentage of your final score for that subject depending on whether you do SL or HL. Check these out and be honest with yourself. If you feel like you will not put that much effort into your IA, or that you will probably struggle with the IA no matter how hard you try, choose the option where the IA will impact your score less. Alternatively, if you find exams very stressful, take some pressure off yourself ahead of time by choosing subjects with a large internally assessed component, and bag yourself marks before you've even walked into the exam hall.

Regarding exams, HL students have to complete either an extra exam paper or spend more time and answer more questions than SL students. While this means you have to study more and know a wider part of the course in depth, it also means that you spread the risk, as each individual question or paper is less heavily weighted than with SL. This certainly saved me when I did my History HL exams, with Paper 3 (HL only) making up for my poor Paper 2. Don't forget, though, that HL exam and IA rubrics are stricter (who would have guessed?!), so your work has to be of a higher standard across all components.

That's all for now. Look into your options and choose wisely, but don't overthink it, really. And if you get a fortnight into your IB studies and realise you have made a terrible mistake, speak with your family and then your IB Coordinator as soon as possible- many schools allow students to swap their subjects around at the very beginning of IB1!

2.6.3a What level of Maths should you choose in the IB?

So, you have picked the DP, and you have chosen most of the subjects you really do -- and do not -- want to focus on for the next two years. Now you must decide on the level of study you want to take on in each subject. Maths has the widest range of levels offered in the IB- so how should you choose between them?

When it comes to Maths, you currently have three main options: Maths Studies, Maths Standard Level (SL), and Maths Higher Level (HL). Please note that this guide will not make reference to Further Maths, as this is not an option offered by the majority of IB World Schools, and is therefore not an option for many students. If you would like further information on Further Maths, please contact your school's IB Coordinator directly. In addition, the IB's proposed changes to Mathematics for first examinations in 2021 are not reflected in this advice, but are discussed in great detail in *2.6.3b*.

There are many influences and considerations to be balanced when choosing your level of IB Maths, from simply the level of love you have for the subject, to future educational and career plans. We decided to ask three members of the EIB Education team why they chose the IB Maths level they did, and what the reality of taking this subject was like...

Why I chose Maths SL *by Ebba*

Growing up I always loved Maths. I can remember getting excited about finally getting to multiply at the end of first grade and choosing to do an Algebra class when I was 15 simply because I genuinely wanted to. The older I got, however, the tougher the different aspects of Maths also got, and I found that whilst I was still quite strong in certain areas, I also struggled with others, such as probability.

When it came to choosing Maths in the IB, it was not an easy decision. I briefly toyed with the idea of doing Maths HL, because I thought I might enjoy the challenge. I knew however, that my future ambitions of studying International Relations would not require Maths HL, and there were other subjects far more suited for me to choose as my HLs, such as History and English Language & Literature. This was how I excluded Maths HL from my decision-making process.

It then came down to Maths Studies or Maths SL. Maths Studies was rumoured to be the easier of the two – with greater focus on statistics and probability, whereas Maths SL had greater focus on calculus and trigonometry. As earlier mentioned however, I genuinely had always enjoyed Maths at school, and this tiny thought in the back of my head kept ringing "what if you change your future career plans and suddenly need Maths..." I think it was this that made me decide to do Maths SL – finding that middle ground between what potentially a future career might require and what might have been a (*relatively*) easy 7.

Was it the right decision?

In the end I ended up with a 5 in Maths SL in the IB Diploma, contributing to my 35 points overall. I went on to study Politics and Diplomacy, two degrees that did not require a strong Mathematical background knowledge and I can admit I have not touched a graphic calculator since my IB Maths exam! So my decision not to do Maths HL was spot on. And my decision to do Maths SL over Studies had no greater impact – perhaps I could have got an additional point had I chosen Maths Studies instead, but there is no way of ever knowing that, and it would not have affected my university degree choices either – hence yes, it was the right decision. I enjoyed what I learned and am pleased to at least know that there is a sin, cos and tan out there, despite not using trigonometry in my day-to-day life!

Why I chose Maths HL *by Tim*

Growing up, I was always a strong Maths student, but an all-rounder academically. I feel very fortunate to have attended an IB school as I would have struggled to narrow my studies down to only 3 or 4 subjects at the age of 16 and feel I thrived in an environment which allowed me to pursue all of my academic interests.

As I got older and finished my IGCSEs, my interests slowly moved towards science and computers. Whilst I was a strong Maths student, I certainly wasn't the best in the class. When investigating my university options, I toyed with Computer Science and Economics (amongst others), but ultimately landed on Engineering. I loved building things, coding projects, and generally understanding how things worked. I loved the elegance of Maths but was even more enthralled by the possibilities of science, Physics in particular, which resulted in aeroplanes, enormous subterranean tunnels, and computers. I knew I needed to take Maths HL before entering the IB as most Engineering courses I was considering, both in the UK and the US, suggested 6s/7s for both HL Maths and Physics.

People build up a big aversion to advanced Maths in many western cultures, but I really enjoyed the journey. My HLs of Maths, Physics, and Economics all complemented each other quite nicely, and SL Computer Science meant that virtually all of my subjects played off one another, each contributing to my understand in another and centring my understanding of each within a wider academic context.

I did find the course quite difficult, especially at the beginning, as in order to achieve the top marks in HL Maths you don't only need an analytical brain, but a patient and creative approach to problem solving, which can only come with practice. I had always relied on ability until that point, rarely working very hard in school and suddenly I was putting in extra hours just to keep up with the pace. I had a bit of a *eureka* moment at the end of my 1st year of IB, studying for my mocks, where lots of the more difficult topics in HL Maths - Proof by induction for example - suddenly just made sense. I enjoyed the course the whole way through, and though I was blessed with an excellent teacher, I also put my success in the course down to a methodical approach to studying – revising each component of the syllabus individually, searching for external resources, and reinforcing my areas of weakness through repetition of difficult questions. My strong mathematical foundation meant that I found HL Physics relatively 'easy' and I certain benefited from the analytical methodology I could take across to Economics, my Extended Essay, and more.

I was a bit spooked by Maths HL Paper 1 as my very first IB exam, and ultimately narrowly missed out on my 7 for HL Maths (and a 45 overall!) by 0.2% after, but I'm so glad to have taken the course. I went on to study Engineering Science at Oxford, and I found much of the Maths in the first year course to be on par with the IB HL course, so it prepared me extremely well!

Why I chose Maths Studies *by Babette*

I've always preferred creative and qualitative subjects. Maths was never of particular interest to me, instead the arts and humanities were much more interesting. The idea of spending time indoors for hours struggling over questions that had only one right answer didn't seem appealing - I preferred to spend my time thinking, getting inspired and using my own thoughts and ideas.

In my IGCSEs I actually did quite well in Maths, scoring an A in the final exam. I had the option to do Maths SL if I wanted to, but I felt no inclination to because I preferred to spend more time in other subject areas. At the time I wanted to go to art school, so I also knew that doing Maths Studies wouldn't affect my application in a bad way. Even though I ended up leaving art school and choosing to study Geography, I never regretted taking Studies because I knew I'd never choose a subject at university level that requires a high level of Maths anyway.

Math studies was straightforward and practical, and I actually ended up using what I learnt in Statistics for Geography later on! I know that students who take Studies often get labelled a certain way by other students (I know I was!), but if you know you're not interested in Maths and will not need it later on in life then why would you spend more time than you need to studying it, and potentially jeopardising precious IB points?

For me, Maths Studies was a great option and helped me achieve the points I needed to get into University College London (UCL) for Geography.

As you will see from our examples above, choosing the right level is very much an individual thing- and our profiles will not have touched on even a fragment of the reasons students will provide for their IB Maths choices. You will have to take into consideration what you are hoping to achieve from the course as well as your passion for the subject. If you are considering a degree in Engineering or a similar subject, such as Tim, your university will most likely require you to take Maths HL.

Similarly, certain degrees such as Economics will require Maths SL which might make your decision a little bit easier. You might find, as Babette did, that Maths Studies came in handy for her future degree at university, despite it not being an entrance requirement.

If you will not be choosing a degree that requires a high level of Mathematical knowledge, then your decision will come down to your own passion for the subject and the type of challenge you wish to set yourself and how you hope Maths will play a part alongside your other subject choices.

2.6.3b The New Maths syllabus

IB is launching a whole new syllabus for Maths to be implemented from classes starting in 2019. It seems nothing like the system we have now, so how is this likely to affect students, schools, and even university and college applications?

It's first important to look at the new changes being implemented and examine the differences when compared to our current system. There will be two subjects in Group 5, both of which will be offered in SL and HL:

Mathematics: Analysis and approaches

- "construction of mathematical arguments and develop strong skills in mathematical thinking"
- "real and abstract applications"
- "mathematical problem solving and generalization"

Mathematics: Applications and interpretation

- "developing mathematics for describing our world, modelling and solving practical problems using the power of technology"
- "mathematics seen in a practical context"

Assessments

- SL students: two externally assessed written papers and the internal assessment
- HL students: three externally assessed written papers and the internal assessment

There are some more changes brought into the syllabus. Most noticeably, Mathematical studies (SL) and Further mathematics (HL) are no longer available. For students who would have taken Mathematical studies SL, Applications and interpretation SL course is designed to be most applicable.

There are also no more optional topics available for higher level students. Some of the topics that are currently available as HL options will be introduced as topics in HL of the two new maths subjects. Calculus options will be included in Mathematics: Analysis and approaches HL, and statistics and discrete options will be included in Mathematics: Applications and interpretation HL.

Schools are likely to have four separate classes for Analysis and approaches SL and HL and Applications and interpretation SL and HL. Teachers will need to familiarise themselves with the new syllabus and the different assessment methods.

Regarding university choices, students applying to courses that previously required Mathematics HL will need to take the Mathematics: Analysis and approaches course. Students applying to other courses which do not require maths as a necessary subject will be sufficiently prepared by the Mathematics: Applications and interpretation course. It is likely that universities will recognise the significant change in the IB maths syllabus and set new requirements for subject and level for particular courses where necessary.

2.6.4 Third-Culture Kids and the IB

Personal insights from Ebba, Head of Courses at EIB Education.

In 1997, at the age of seven, my life changed forever. My parents took a big leap and made the decision to relocate our family to the other side of the world and move from a small town in Sweden where they had built a life together and I had always known as "home". The destination was Singapore – a country I had never heard of before, and all I knew was that it was a long way from Sweden.

My parents were excited – and therefore us children, my siblings and I, were also excited. My parents had been over to visit in the spring and picked out our new schools and found a place for us to live. The big news was that we would have a communal pool in the garden – something which for a seven year old who has been brought up in the cold northern country of Sweden was more important than anything else!

Selling our childhood home in Sweden, we bought an old summer house not far away which until this day is our base "in the world". Whilst my father flew out at the start of the summer to start his new job, we followed him three months later at the start of August. To entertain us on the long flight, my younger brother and I had a brand new Gameboy with the games Super Mario and Tetris, which we had to share on the flight so whilst one of us played the other could sleep or watch one of the on-board films. It was an exciting journey and an exciting time!

Arriving to a new country, we found ourselves as expats for the first time ever. I was in a class with children from countries from around the world, where one of the main days to celebrate in school was International Day where everyone would come dressed in the colour of their home country's flag or national dress and bring in food from one's country to share. My friends were from Singapore, Norway, the US, Thailand, and Ireland, to name just a few.

The first time I came across the International Baccalaureate was when I was about ten years old and some of the older Swedes at my school, United World College of Southeast Asia were starting their first IBDP year. It was also around this time that I knew that this could be the route I would look to pursue through my own later studies. I remember my mother telling me that it was a system of education which I would be able to follow anywhere in the world, whether in Singapore or back home in Sweden, and, having got a taste for living abroad and travelling the world, this sounded like the perfect route to go down, even in the mind of a ten year old.

Interestingly enough, all of my future schools in one way or another had an IB connection. After four years in Singapore, our family packed our bags and travelled back across the world, this time relocating to Luxembourg. Here I also attended an IB school, but was still too young to actually start the Diploma myself. All of the older, cooler kids who I looked up to were in their final two years and I remember clearly observing how many of them were applying to universities around the world, including the UK.

A few years and countries later, I found myself for the first time as a student on a completely different, non-IB, curriculum. After completing my Pre-IB year at a small international school in Sweden, I decided to go to the US for a year as an exchange student at an American High School in Kentucky. It was a great experience to try a different mix of subjects which I would not be able to take at home, such as drama, art and American History – I even signed up for pre-calculus. Despite the opportunity to finish school one year early, it was etched on my mind that I would go back home after a year, and complete the IB rather than having the junior year of my American High School experience count towards my final school grades. The question was just where I would go to school. And the beauty of the IB, as previously mentioned, is that it can be completed anywhere. My parents, having moved to Switzerland, proposed me coming out there to do it but alternatively I could chose to remain in Sweden and do my two final years there, allowing me to choose Swedish as one of my main languages. I chose the latter option and got the chance to finish the IB, a truly international programme, whilst also taking part in the Swedish graduation tradition, the famous "*studenten*"!

I graduated from my IB studies in 2008. And with a decade's worth of hindsight, I can say that it is one of the greatest academic achievements to have completed the IB diploma. I hold a Bachelor's Degree in Politics and a Master's Degree in Diplomacy and truly do not think I could have been better prepared for these degrees than what the IB made me. From analysing concepts to being able to look at problems from many different angles, the IB has the ability to teach students lots of knowledge whilst also passing on the skills of how to apply it and understanding why something is the case.

Even to this day I come across other former IB students, and often I find we at one point or another went to the same school somewhere else in the world. Because that is the beautiful thing about the IB – it is a fantastic academic network, extending far and wide across the world, clearly showing that if you were once an IB student, you will always be proud to have been an IB student and be connected to the international world in a way which is difficult to come by elsewhere.

IB Resources & Events

You can find even more IB resources - including videos, articles, FAQs and more - on our website at

eibeducation.com/resources

3.
How to succeed in the IB

3. How to succeed in the IB

3.1 Study tips

Success in your IB comes down to organisation. At the beginning of each term check whether certain periods will be deadline heavy, so that you can plan to give yourself enough time to complete coursework. Set yourself personal deadlines to draft essays ahead of time, and always allow a day or two to review just in case. The good news is, we have done the majority of this planning for you! Keep track of the IB external and internal assessment deadlines with our Year Planner (see 5.1)!

The IB exams, while changing year-on-year, tend to use the same command terms and will expect the application of knowledge contained within the course materials and syllabus, which means they be formulaic in terms of the types of questions that are asked and what is expected of you. Through the syllabus, mark schemes, and past papers, you can 'crack the code' of how the exams work. Of course, even the best code-crackers can't beat hard work! See below for our subject-specific revision tips, written by IB graduates who worked hard and achieved exceptionally well in each of the following areas- although it is fair to say we all made a mistake at some point or another, we hope you will find our advice useful nonetheless!

3.2.1 Group 1

English

Whether you are preparing for your final exams in English Literature or Language & Literature, there are key ways to reduce stress during revision, and to even, hopefully, make revision fun!

Your teacher will have selected works, text types, and genres, to not only provide an interesting and varied literary education, but also to make it as easy as possible for you to revise for your final exams, based on their teaching methods. For some teachers, this means poems for both the unseen (P1) and P2, while for others novels with key socioeconomic and historical themes fit their teaching style so they are best placed to help you revise these. Before revising, make sure you understand the **requirements of each paper**, and **why your teacher has selected the texts** they have.

When revising for P2, no matter the text type selected by your teacher, you will be faced with a mountain of notes, quotes, and arguments to sort and memorise. **Do not try to memorise whole essays!** Instead, work through your texts and mind-map all the themes which they have in common, and where there are differences. You will also need to identify key characters and relationships in prose, and understand the position of the speaker and any characters in poetry. You will definitely need your terminology down, giving you a clear understanding of the definition of all your key terms but also great examples of these from your texts. Be canny! If nature as a theme appears through several of your texts, identify metaphors and imagery which draw on the natural world so that you are using the same technical terminology for several texts at once. Also memorise some contextual information for each text, such that if the worst happens and you draw a blank when planning your essay response you at least have something you can easily write down to get your brain moving!

Practise makes perfect - **do every past paper** you can get your hands on, but do them in timed conditions, and aim to mimic exam conditions as far as possible- which means hand writing responses regularly for an extended period before your exam- you do not want an out of practise writing hand on exam day! Once you have run out of time, stop, and leave the paper for at least 24 hours before you come to mark it. This should prevent you from giving yourself 'I know what I was trying to say' marks, as while your point might be beautifully salient inside your own head, the examiner only has access to what you really write on the day! Set yourself measurable targets to improve your essays to avoid the frustration of marking subjective papers- if you struggle to include sufficient close analysis in your essays, give yourself a minimum number of key terms to include per essay. If your essays are too descriptive, set a maximum number of words allocated to 'filler', or paragraph transitions.

Plan every essay, and plan more than you think anyone has ever planned before. In the exam, you shouldn't be making new connections between texts in the middle of a paragraph- it is very likely that you'll think of new points during the exam, but go back to your plan and find the best place for them, rather than shoehorning them into your current paragraph. Keep as much of your creative mind free during the exam to focus on argumentation and a beautiful essay, rather than trying to closely analyse a text under pressure.

Tutor Content
We asked Tom, one of our English and History tutors, to provide his advice on preparing for the oft-dreaded unseen P1 for English, both in the Literature and the Language/Literature courses:

How to write a Language commentary
Learning to write a good commentary is one of the most valuable things about the IB English Literature course, because the ability to understand the message of a text and the skill to perceive the uses and constructions of language will prove useful to students throughout their lives.

Paper 1 tests these skills by giving students 90 or 120 minutes to write a commentary on a choice of a poem or a piece of prose. The IB examines on the basis of four criteria, all of which it is essential to appreciate.

Criterion A: Understanding and Interpretation
The IB are looking for an excellent **overall appreciation** of the text: its main message, the central purpose of the author, as well as an understanding of its basic features. You should demonstrate this from the very first sentence of the commentary.

Criterion B: Appreciation of the Writer's Choices
Throughout your commentary, you should bear this criterion in mind. Try not to stray too far into the broad themes of the passage; the examiners are always looking for a focus on the linguistic features of the text, and the exact techniques by which the author is conveying their overall meaning.

Criterion C: Organization and Development
You should avoid a line-by-line approach to your commentary: instead organise your paragraphs around specific themes and features of the text.

Criterion D: Language
Write in a formal fashion, using as much precise vocabulary as possible. Avoid slang and make sure you quote frequently from the passage – around three times each paragraph.

Writing the commentary in **14 steps**
1) Decide on the poem or the prose. You should aim to practice both so you are comfortable doing either, but it is natural for students to have a preference. Pick the text with the most substance you feel you can comment on in an intelligent manner. I often chose poems since they are complete expressions and not an extract from a larger work. Spend a maximum of 5 minutes making this decision.

2) Give an initial reading of your chosen passage and try to identify its overall message. Helpful

questions you can ask yourself at this stage are: What is the essence of the text? What meaning is the author trying to convey? What is the central emotional resonance?

3) Spend some time thinking about this, and then formulate a thesis statement: a single sentence that states very clearly your exact impression of the text.

4) Go over the text, this time asking yourself the question: how is the author accomplishing this aim? This should not be an attempt to spot features randomly, but considering how language has been used to fulfil the essential meaning of the text. Annotate thoroughly, scouring the text for as many different linguistic devices that serve your thesis statement.

5) After about five minutes of close reading, you should hopefully have found three or four major linguistic areas. Select three quotations from each of these areas and organise them under headings: e.g. natural imagery, fatalistic symbolism and irony.

6) Now you are ready to begin your plan. Write your full thesis statement. For example: 'throughout the poem Shakespeare seeks to do eternal justice to the person he loves through the medium of verse, and achieves this through the extended metaphor of 'a summer's day', rich natural imagery and a masterful use of the sonnet form'. The thesis statement should combine your overall impression of the passage with a precise indication of the three main linguistic areas you are going to focus on.

7) Now plan each of your three paragraphs. Ideally you will select three quotations, one from the beginning, middle and end of your text, demonstrating an appreciation for the device across the passage and noting any differences or developments. For each quotation, write a few words in your plan that will prompt you to analyse the language of the quotation directly.

Overall this will mean around nine quotations, each of which you will analyse in turn throughout your commentary.

8) Try and find good linking sentences between these paragraphs as you plan them, rather than beginning each paragraph with 'Another aspect of the text is...;' Using good conjoining sentences will make your commentary seem more than the sum of its parts and help you fulfil Criterion C.

9) Once you have completed this for all your paragraphs, you are ready to start writing! You should spend around 30 minutes on your plan: this may seem like a lot but it will mean that when you come to writing the commentary you will be able to do so much more fluently and will save yourself time.

10) Begin the commentary with some brief context about the passage, no more than a sentence. The introduction should not be very long, consisting of a first sentence outlining the basic action and context of the passage. The next sentence should be your thesis statement, which should be stated in a precise and clear manner. Then outline the three main areas you will be focusing on, indicating the approach you will take. Try and avoid vague descriptions like 'structure, form, tone' but instead add more descriptive adjectives that show you have a more subtle appreciation of these devices: e.g. 'chiasmatic structure, iambic tetrameters, existential tone.'

11) Next, go into your first paragraph. Think of each paragraph as being a mini-essay. Just as the introduction serves as the basis from which the rest of your essay is expanded, each paragraph should unfold neatly from its opening sentence. Therefore each of your quotations should merely be illustrations of the point you make in your opening sentence. Make sure you analyse the specific language of each quotation, remembering each time to connect those thoughts to the message of your thesis

statement.

12) In between each paragraph, try to use as many connecting sentences as possible. If, for example, the sarcastic tone of a poem is conveyed through its rhythm, use this connection as the start of your next paragraph.

13) As you progress through the commentary, remember to quote frequently from the text. Keep the quotations short so you can go into lots of details about the techniques being used.

14) Your conclusion, much like your introduction, should not be very long. Hopefully the process of writing the commentary has prompted you to think something in addition to your original thesis statement. Perhaps there is greater subtlety you wish to add at this stage. Make one additional comment on the text overall and then recap the main areas you have written about. End with a direct reference to your original thesis statement.

Depending on how quickly you write, you may choose to write more than three main paragraphs. Anything up to five paragraphs can work well with this structure, and you can continue to add different points to your commentary. The most important thing is to demonstrate that you understand what the text is about, how the writer has achieved this, and that you structure your essay vary clearly and in a coherent and connected fashion, according to different themes using appropriate technical language.

How to write an SL Language & Literature commentary

Many students, both HL and SL, come to us for assistance with Paper 1, the unseen aspect of the IB Language and Literature course. This advice aims to address some of the most common concerns and to provide students with a highly useful method to write the ideal commentary.

The biggest difference between SL and HL is that you only have to write a commentary on a single piece at Standard Level. The IB selects a diverse range of sources for Paper 1 extracts so the key here is flexibility. This adaptability is something you can acquire by doing lots of practice on different types of text, going above and beyond the mocks you do with your teacher. It is very important to appreciate the IB's assessment criteria when thinking about how to structure your commentary. These are broken down below.

Criterion A: Understanding and Interpretation
The IB are looking for an excellent **overall appreciation** of the text: its main message, the central purpose of the author, as well as an

understanding of its basic features. You should aim to show this at the very beginning of your commentary, and this should be the first thing you are trying to understand about the text when you read it for the first time.

Criterion B: Appreciation of the Writer's Choices

Throughout your commentary, you should bear this criterion in mind. Try not to stray too far into the broad themes of the passage because the examiners are always looking for a **focus on the linguistic features of the text**, and the exact techniques by which the author is conveying their overall meaning.

Criterion C: Organization and Development

You should **avoid a line-by-line approach** to your commentary: instead organise your paragraphs around specific themes and features of the text.

Criterion D: Language

Write in a formal fashion, using as much precise vocabulary as possible. Avoid slang and make sure you quote frequently from the passage – around three times each paragraph.

Writing the commentary in **14 steps**

1) When you open the paper, look at each of the extracts and decide which text you will focus on. You should aim to practice various different types (articles, adverts, travel writing etc.) so you are comfortable with them, but it is natural for students to have a preference. Pick the text with the most substance you feel you can comment on in an intelligent manner. Spend a maximum of 5 minutes making this decision.

2) Give an initial reading of your chosen passage and try to identify its overall message. Helpful questions you can ask yourself at this stage are: What is the essence of the text? What meaning is the author trying to convey? What is the central emotional resonance? What can you infer about the context?

3) Spend some time thinking about this, and then formulate a thesis statement: a single sentence that states very clearly your exact impression of the text. Think of this as the what section of your commentary.

4) Go over the text, this time asking yourself the question: how is the author accomplishing this aim? This should not be an attempt to spot features randomly, but considering how language has been used to fulfil the essential meaning of the text. Annotate thoroughly, scouring the text for as many different linguistic devices that serve your thesis statement as you can.

5) After about five minutes of close reading, you should hopefully have found three or four major linguistic areas. Select three quotations from each of these areas and organise them under headings, trying to add adjectives before them to make your points more specific: e.g. sensationalist language, use of juxtaposing quotations and erratic structure.

6) Now you are ready to begin your plan. Write your full thesis statement. For example: 'throughout the article the author performs a subtle piece of satire that ridicules the current US President comprehensively, and this is achieved through the use of dark humour, effective linguistic motifs and a simple structure.' The thesis statement should combine your overall impression of the passage with a precise indication of the three main linguistic areas you are going to focus on.

7) Now plan each of your three paragraphs. Ideally you will select three quotations, one from the beginning, middle and end of your text, demonstrating an appreciation for the device across the passage and noting any differences or developments. For each quotation, write a few words in your plan that will prompt you to analyse the language of the quotation directly.

Overall this will mean around nine quotations, each of which you will analyse in turn throughout your commentary.

8) Try and find good linking sentences between these paragraphs as you plan them, rather than beginning each paragraph with 'Another aspect of the text is...;' Using good conjoining sentences will make your commentary seem more than the sum of its parts and help you fulfil Criterion C.

9) Once you have completed this for all your paragraphs, you are ready to start writing! You should spend around 30 minutes on your plan: this may seem like a lot but it will mean that when you come to writing the commentary you will be able to do so much more fluently and will save yourself time.

10) Begin the commentary with some brief context about the passage, no more than a few sentences. After that should be your thesis statement, which should be stated in a precise and clear manner. Then outline the three main areas you will be focusing on, indicating the approach you will take, remembering to include precise adjectives.

11) Next, go into your first paragraph. Think of each paragraph as being a mini-essay. Just as the introduction serves as the basis from which the rest of your essay is expanded, each paragraph should unfold neatly from its opening sentence. Therefore each of your quotations should merely be illustrations of the point you make in your opening sentence. Make sure you analyse the specific language of each quotation, remembering each time to connect those thoughts to the message of your thesis statement.

12) In between each paragraph, try to use as many connecting sentences as possible. If, for example, the sarcastic tone of an article is conveyed through its structure, use this as the bridge between those two paragraphs.

13) As you progress through the commentary, remember to quote frequently from the text. Keep the quotations short so you can go into lots of details about the techniques being used.

14) Your conclusion, much like your introduction, should not be very long. Hopefully the process of writing the commentary has prompted you to think something in addition to your original thesis statement. Perhaps there is greater subtlety you wish to add at this stage. Make one additional comment on the text overall and then recap the main areas you have written about. End with a direct reference to your original thesis statement.
The more you practice, the more you will feel able to write four or five paragraphs in your commentary. This is absolutely fine, and the same method suggested here can also be used.

 How to write a HL Language & Literature commentary

This is a great chance to display your skills in comparison and contrast, something you will be familiar with from other parts of the IB.

Assessment Criteria
The main difference with the HL criteria is Criterion A: Understanding and comparison of the texts:
Level 5 – *'There is excellent understanding of the texts, their context and purpose, and the similarities and differences between them; comments are fully supported by well-chosen references to the texts.'*

A lot of the method for planning and structuring the commentary at HL is similar to the SL method, so what follows is some useful advice on how to Compare and Contrast.

1) Always organise your paragraphs around particular themes and features of the text.

2) Focus on the points of similarity in these themes within each paragraph, and then move on to discussing the differences. You should avoid writing a commentary that deals entirely with one passage and then another, since the IB are looking for a coherent structure that can synthesises both passages into a single effective commentary.

3) In your paragraphs, remember always to directly analyse any language that you quote. This should involve some comment on **the way in which the author's language is shaping their meaning, and also the effects on the reader**.

4) You should always use the guiding questions that the IB gives as part of the Paper 1 question, but be sure to be more precise than this when you are structuring your essay. In your introduction it can be tempting to follow the guiding questions broadly and write something like, 'and this is achieved through the use of tone' but this is actually rather imprecise and not what the examiners are looking for. It is absolutely fine to use these prompts in your commentary, but always be sure to specify the way in which this feature has been used rather than just a generic reference. Therefore, rephrase it in your introduction by saying, for example, that you will discuss the use of 'sardonic tone'.

5) Try to infer as much about the context as possible: the date of the publication, the information in the passage, your own knowledge about what is being discussed. Use this to inform your ideas about who the readership of the text might be, and therefore the effects that certain techniques might have on these readers.

6) Finally, remember to keep quoting directly from both texts. Avoid going off into broad comparisons between ideas in both texts, and remember to keep your commentary grounded in the language that is being used, and the relationship that has to the overall meaning of the text.

For both HL and SL, your commentary is going to be a thread of individual points. For each of these, you should always make sure to make your **point**, provide a **quotation** and then give some linguistic **analysis**.

The best chance you can have of success in this subject is to do multiple full practice commentaries, and also many more practice plans.

3.2.2 Group 2

Language Acquisition (B)

It seems difficult to get better at languages, especially when exams start coming up close and you start to feel like you're running out of time. But you *can* get better, if you learn to familiarise yourself with the language. Try to expose yourself to a little bit each day, for example by reading the news, listening to podcasts, watching TV shows, or even listening to music in the target language. Find something you enjoy so you'll keep doing it every day. See what you can find and let your brain get used to the language so it doesn't freak out when it sees an whole exam paper written in it.

During your studies / before your exam

- Use past papers. Do the same thing you do with other subjects: create an exam-like environment and practice timing. The one thing you can do differently is highlighting any words you don't know, especially if they keep popping up. Once you've finished a past paper, take a break then come back to it to make a list of words you didn't know, including their meaning.

- Try to spend 5-10 minutes every day to read over the list. You don't have to sit down until you've memorised the words completely, but simply becoming familiar with them will be helpful. Similar words come up in exams every year, and so it's very likely the words you learned will come up.
- Do the same during class and highlight or make note of any words you don't know. Make a different list with these words. You don't need to prioritise them as much as words from past papers, but they'll still be useful to know.
- In Paper 2, similar topics come up again and again, so find a pattern and practice questions that come up often but that you also feel confident with. Your actual exam will feel much more familiar and comfortable, and you're likely to have answered a similar question during your practices.

During the exam

- Before you start answering any questions, read over all the texts first and underline words you don't know. You might be able to remember some of them later on.
- Your answers will be within the text. Find them directly in the text before answering your questions.
- As you're reading texts, don't assume meanings of words you don't know. When a questions asks material related to the word, read your answer options first then carefully think about what the word might mean. Think logically and don't jump into conclusions.
- With Paper 2, read all questions and topics first and pick some you feel confident with. Make a quick outline for each before you decide the one you'd like to pursue with.
- Once you find a topic you like, make a more detailed outline while also taking note of the word count. Plan approximately how many words you can afford to write in each paragraph. The word count will also be useful for timing your exam.

- As you write, it might be useful to count your words after each paragraph to keep track of how many words you still have to write while also checking your timing. Check if your actual word count aligns with your planned one.
- When you're finished writing, make sure you've left enough time to read it over. Look for mistakes, especially grammar ones. Read over each word carefully to check if the verb form / gender of noun / preposition is used correctly. Also make sure you have not exceeded the word count.

Written assignment (HL)

- Summer's the best time to read books. In those few months you have, pick your books, try to finish them and make a decision on which one you want to write about.
- Make notes while reading. Write down quotes or specific details that you think might be important for your assignment.
- Try to think about possible topics and themes related to your book. Keep several in mind and try to think about how you could potentially expand on each of them.

Internal assessment (oral)

- If there's anyone you can practice speaking to, use the opportunity and practice as often as you can. You don't have to spend hours in a single day, but try to meet them as often as possible to have short conversations.
- It might be difficult or even impossible to find someone to speak the language to. Don't worry and focus on practicing listening instead. Find podcasts or shows that interest you and listen to them in the bus or while relaxing at home. You don't have to understand everything you hear, but get your ears used to listening to the language.

Language ab initio

You can take a huge variety of languages on the IB. Here we've chosen to focus on French, but much of the advice here is valid for most languages!

French is a particularly difficult language to master at any level. Here are a few tips to help you master IB French at *ab initio* level.

Studying IB French *ab initio* can be quite difficult, since you will be learning the language from scratch (or almost). Knowing how to tackle French from the first day will be a huge advantage, so here are a few things you can do to boost your French, or other *ab initio* language learning.

Learn, don't memorise:

When studying a language at school, some people just try to memorise entire paragraphs and hope they can use them in the exam. But that's the opposite of what you should be doing - you should learn the language if you want to do well. The best way to learn French is to immerse yourself in the language; you will have to speak, listen, read and write in French. And no, you don't need to live in a French-speaking country to do so.

- Speaking: Practise speaking with your classmates, or, even better, with a friend who is in French B or A. It might be hard and your conversations won't be great, but you can help each other and become more confident speakers. Of course, try to talk to your French teacher in French only - the point is to get your brain and mouth used to this new set of sounds and shapes.
- Listening: Listen to songs in French with lyrics, watch videos in French, and if you are confident enough, try watching a movie or a show in French. Put on subtitles, since the point is that you begin understanding what is going on. As you become more confident, switch the subtitle language to French so that you can relate how words are spelled and how they are pronounced - which is vital, since many French words are pronounced very differently to how they are spelled.
- Reading: Try to read children's books in French. If you consider yourself too mature for that, remember that several literary classics have been adapted for children - so check those out

for a more interesting read with words you will understand. If reading books isn't for you, you can search online for news for children in French, which will keep you both up to date with current events and your French studies.

- Writing: Your teacher will give you loads of written tasks to practise, but if you want to go the extra mile then you could keep a journal and write about your day, or anything you'd like, in French. Start with simple sentences and gradually add what you learn in school. You will make loads of mistakes, so it is important for you to try to proofread what you write and find mistakes. If your teacher is willing to proofread your journal, then take advantage of that opportunity.

Visual Stimuli:

French grammar is very complicated, so learning all its tricks can be difficult. To help you study, write/highlight using different colours. For example, write male nouns in blue, female ones in red, and so on. This will make you more aware of how French is written, and let's admit it, it will make your writing look more jazzy and exciting.

Daily revision:

This is the rule nobody likes to follow, but it's essential with languages. Revise as often as possible. As mentioned earlier, as long as you read or watch videos in French, you will be revising. You don't need to sit down in front of a textbook!

Past Papers:

It's very important for you to understand the format of exams and what each paper asks of you, so you should practice with past papers before exams. Paper 1 is all about understanding texts, so familiarise yourself with the different format and writing styles these texts come in. You will be writing your own texts in Paper 2, so make sure you know what to include in every format they might ask you (for example, if you need to write a letter, don't forget to write the address).

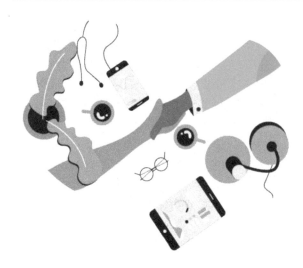

3.3.3 Group 3

Business Management

Whether it's mocks or final IB exams coming up, revision can be a very stressful time. If you're studying Business Management, you will face an extensive syllabus full of terminology, case studies and even some Maths. The BM exams can be tricky, but don't worry; we have some tips for you to ace your Business exams, whether you are in SL or HL.

Schedule your revision time:

You should do this for all your subjects. If you allocate a number of hours per day, you will be more likely to do the hardest part of revising, which is actually sitting down to study. Plan when you should finish revising a topic and start the next one, but don't forget to schedule breaks and free time too. With goals and deadlines to meet, your revision will be more productive.

Know your keywords:

Like most IB subjects, BM has a lot of terminology and definitions you should know. A common problem, especially in finance questions, is that students can't answer a question because they don't understand what the question is asking them to find out or define. You don't need to memorise the exact definition, but make sure you study and understand every concept and technicality.

Know your exams:

SL and HL exams are slightly different, so you should be aware of what your exam will look like and how many questions you need to answer. Both SL and HL have to complete 2 papers.

Paper 1 is based on a case study which will be given to you in advance. Make sure you read the case study, highlight all the important parts and analyse it (e.g. who are the stakeholders? What are the business objectives?, and so on). Do not try to memorise answers to possible questions - it's tempting, but if the exam asks you for something you haven't prepared for, you will not do well. Instead, make sure you know the case study's issues so you can apply it when answering the questions.

Meanwhile, Paper 2's infamous aspect is Section C, which requires you to write an essay based on a real-life company and the impact upon it of two of the following six aspects: change, culture, ethics, globalisation, innovation, and strategy. You'll have to be knowledgeable of a company, but don't prioritise memorising random figures - they may look great and could improve your answer, but they won't count for much if you can't apply them to the question. Instead, study your company in relation to the six elements and use relevant information and facts to bolster your report.

Past Papers & Timing:

Doing past paper questions is as helpful as studying the whole syllabus. Time yourself when completing a full paper so you can see how much time you need per section. Also, look at the marks given per question; the smaller the number, the less time you should spend doing them and the less detailed they have to be. As always, don't forget to bring a watch to the exam to make sure you finish on time!

History

IB History is a very intense course with **loads** of material to study, so having a good revision strategy is vital for the exams.

Take notes in class & study in advance:

You simply cannot cram the entire History course the night before the exam- please don't try! You should begin to revise well in advance - and if you study a bit throughout the two years, most facts should stick in your head by the time you need to revise for your final exams, saving you loads of study time. This also means that you should be taking well-presented, clear, and detailed notes in class or at home throughout the two years to make your revision easier. The last thing you want to do is have no notes or incomplete notes when you sit down for your revision, so do be sure to check your notes at the end of each topic to ensure you will be able to revise from these when the time comes.

Flashcards & Timelines:

A great way to memorise all the dates and events is to make your own flashcards and timelines. Timelines take more time to create but can be the a better option, since you can see what was happening at each point in time and how events progressed, which will allow you to analyse your topics in a more global context, making your understanding of history more elaborate. You might even notice connections between seemingly unrelated topics by seeing if they happened during similar time periods or in similar circumstances.

Essay Practice:

Memorising dates won't be enough to get a good mark in History (though it is an important aspect!). Your essay skills need to be perfect for Paper 2 (and Paper 3 if you are doing HL). There are three main things you can do to improve your essay-writing skills:

1. Outlines: You don't really need to write a million essays to practice (although it's a good idea to do several timed essays before the exam to practice time-management). Writing down outlines of your answer will help you organise your work, structure your arguments, and bring in all the relevant evidence you need in each paragraph. This will help you improve your structure, which is vital for essays, and will also help to recall dates and events.

2. Critical thinking: IB History essays are *argumentative* essays, meaning that you need to have a viewpoint on an issue, and then analyse

and evaluate it. Do not spend too much time describing events. Focus on *why* your evidence supports your claim - but also think of its limitations and possible counterarguments. You need to be critical of your work if you want to achieve a 7. Purely descriptive essays will not score highly, as they do not demonstrate the requisite skills and engagement with the historical events, historiography, and opinions presented by any source or question.

3. Break down the question: You should always divide the question into three sections: what it wants you to do (e.g. evaluate), the issue at hand (e.g. rise to power) and the subject (e.g. Lenin). It will make the question easier to understand and you will be able to give an answer which is well-focused on the question.

Sporadic source practice:

Paper 1 is fully based on your ability to analyse sources, so you should take some time throughout the course to check out different sources - from book extracts to satirical cartoons and propaganda. You can analyse the message of a source or compare and contrast it to another one in a relatively short amount of time, and doing this sort of quick practice will certainly boost your source-analysis skills. Obviously, do a proper Paper 1 practice too when the time of the exam comes nearer.

Psychology

The Psychology syllabus is broad in nature, covering the Biological, Cognitive and Sociocultural approaches to understanding behaviour alike, as well as various research methodologies. As such, it can feel as if there is simply too much to learn for the purpose of the exams, not to mention that you also have the options (one for SL and two for HL) to deal with.

A subject with this level of content requires you to be somewhat economical in your revision techniques, though this of course does not mean cutting corners!

Remember that you will need to have a solid understanding of all three approaches in order to answer three compulsory short-answer questions in Section A of Paper 1; there are a total of 27 marks available in this section of the first paper, so in fact, these short-answer questions contribute more to your score here than the essay question (worth 22 marks) does in the latter section of this paper. Therefore, you cannot get away with simply ignoring an entire approach (more on this later), and you will need to know enough about each such that you could confidently define, describe, and explain concepts across these three approaches, backing these answers up with carefully described research where relevant. You do not need to be especially critical or creative with your answers here: it is sufficient to simply have a solid understanding of the material and convey this in a clear and concise manner.

In Section B, you can be somewhat more focused in your approach, given that you are able to select one essay from a choice of three. The paper is structured such that there will always be one question on each of the approaches, though this does *not* mean that you can get away with simply knowing one approach in detail and ignoring the other two for the most part. There is always the risk that a particularly tricky question comes up for a given approach, so you need to have other options available. It is therefore advisable to learn two of the three approaches in depth, with a thorough understanding of each topic, and leave the third simply for short-answer questions (so focus on the most fundamental theories and studies). This should leave you suitably well-prepared that there will always be a question you can tackle.

That said, try to be tactful in your revision: choose research that is representative of the approach as a whole (e.g. the case study of HM excellently illustrates many concepts within both the Biological and Cognitive approaches); it is far better to know a small number of studies and theories in depth (with thorough descriptions and analyses of methodology and conclusions, as well as names and dates!) than to be able to list 30 pieces of research in an essay but discuss them only superficially. There are a total of 22 marks available here, most of which are awarded

for your understanding, use of research, and critical thinking skills (this is where the analysis of a study's methodology comes in). However, a smaller number of marks are also on offer for the extent to which your essay focuses on the question, and the clarity and organisation of your answer, so remember to plan carefully (spend 5-10 minutes doing so) and write clearly and meaningfully!

Geography

So we all know that IB Geography can be a bit of a slippery slope when it comes to revision, but here is how to smash the exams out the water...

While you may have spent 2 years having the time of your life learning about pingos and hanging valleys, when you finally reach exams you will suddenly realise that there are 10,000,000+ definitions and case studies to remember and only 2 days to do it in. At this point your heart will jump into your mouth, causing you to whimper silently and start praying for time to reverse. In short, you will probably wish that you had taken the subject more seriously from the start... at least this was my experience!

Having finished with the (major) nightmare that is the exam period, I know that the final few weeks of revision can hugely stressful. So my number 1 top tip is not to leave anything until the last minute! The key to being successful in any subject at IB level is about being proactive inside and outside of class. You need to be organised, attentive in class and have all your notes from every class neatly organised whether online or in printed form. Keep your notes for each paper (1, 2 & 3) together and within that separate your topics and themes! I promise this will make the start of revision so much less painful and you might even be excited to make your own beautiful filing system!

Right so you are all set. Your final exams start in a couple of months. Now down to the nitty gritty: what should you really pay attention to when it comes to revision?

Top tip number 2: Command Terms are KEY

Command terms are the quickest and easiest way of boosting your marks! Understanding what the exam is asking you to do is a surefire way of making sure whoever is looking at your paper knows you are well informed, well prepared and academically rigorous. No matter how much you know about glaciers, if the question is asking you define a glacier and you explain their formation - you will not get the marks and you will waste time! Make sure you understand the number of marks for each command term and the depth of answer you are required to give.

Top tip 3: Diagrams are your secret weapon

Ever heard the saying 'a picture is worth 1000 words'... well it's not quite the same but in the IB a diagram can be worth a significant number of marks! A well labeled and explained diagram can often be key in successfully answering questions so try and have at least one or two ready-to-go for all your topics. These help not only to show the examiner that you truly understand what you are talking about, but also gives structure to your thoughts around a topic, aids memorisation and makes sure you include everything related to the diagram. When you look at a diagram you have drawn and realise there's an additional line you haven't labeled and discussed - that's when they can save you some sneaky marks!

Top tip 4: Case Studies do not have to be (a) based in the UK, (b) have happened in 500 bc or (c) be the same ones everyone else uses

Sorry for the long title but I think it gets across (if not succinctly) what I'm trying to say...

The best thing about Geography is its relevance to the modern world. Everything you see, hear, smell and sense is Geography in some form or another. Today's world should be the inspiration for your case studies and global and local news is your portal into this. This is particularly helpful for the HL extension course but is 100% applicable to the course as a whole. When you use current affairs for your case studies it achieves 2 key things. First, you become way more interested in your studies; this way you

tend to remember more, have a greater depth of understanding and be more critical in your thinking. Secondly, your essays become 10 times more original and interesting for the examiners. It's a win-win situation.

Top tip 5: Use Past Paper Questions & the Mark Scheme

Geography paper 1 is a saving grace! It's a much easier paper and it is very, very possible to score really highly (even 100%). Questions tend to be quite repetitive year-on-year and this means that if you do loads of past papers and read the mark schemes carefully chances are that you will have seen a question - or at least one like it - before and will know exactly what the examiners are looking for. So get going on those past papers! It could just save you a sweet, *sweet* 7.

Finally my 6th and most exclusive top tip, a little treat for those who have read all the way to the bottom, is that throughout the IB and particularly the revision process you need to remember that Geography can be and should be fun! Geography is an incredibly dynamic and interesting subject that tackles so many important and interesting themes -- such as inequality, globalisation, hazard risk etc. -- and it can be so easy to forget this. But in Geography everything you learn about actually happens around you and is super important in understanding world social, economic and environmental processes. So keep calm and have fun with it!

3.3.4 Group 4

Biology

IB Biology is a content-heavy course, so can feel a little daunting to revise, but can be easily broken down and made much more manageable when you come to tackle it.

Firstly, your syllabus is the most helpful revision tool- it tells you everything you need to know for the exams and, in many cases, what you do not need to! Familiarise yourself with the structure of the course: the number of topics you need to learn (including your option), the suggested teaching hours for each (which gives you an idea of how much revision time to devote to a given topic), and, most importantly, the content of each topic and sub-topic. Pay particular attention to the terms 'Application' and 'Skill' and the associated syllabus points, as these provide some guidance as to what could be asked of you in an exam question (e.g. drawing a diagram, defining a concept, explaining a process).

Once you feel comfortable with the structure of the syllabus, you can start planning your revision accordingly. Begin to prioritise certain topics or subtopics based on your knowledge of your own strengths and weaknesses, refining this over time as you attempt past papers and establish gaps in your understanding. You may feel generally confident in Genetics, but simply need to focus on drawing out Punnett squares to tackle some of the trickier questions within this topic, for instance, so do ensure your revision is targeted to specific subtopics, or even individual syllabus points. Breaking down the syllabus in this way makes it far more manageable, providing handy 'chunks' of learning which you can easily incorporate into your overall revision timetable.

Though knowledge application is essential in approaching any of the IB experimental sciences, Biology is arguably more memory-heavy than some of the other Group 4 subjects, and you will need to be able to recall a significant number of definitions, diagrams, and processes.

Mind maps can be a very effective way of condensing the large amounts of content into an accessible form that you can readily look over the night before the exam; as a highly visual revision tool, they also work excellently with diagrams, and you consider putting them up on your wall to glance at even when you are not immersed in revision! Many students also find flashcards to be a great way of practising definitions - marks easily gained with adequate revision, but easily lost if you are not specific in your choice of terminology.

Finally, remember the importance of past papers, as mentioned above: make sure you know from an early stage what sorts of questions can be asked, and how they might be structured and phrased, as you will inevitably notice some common themes by attempting several papers. The data-based question poses a challenge for many students given that it features content beyond the scope of the syllabus, and relies on your ability to analyse graphs, charts, and diagrams, and to draw conclusions based on this information. As you cannot revise any specific content for this question, practice is especially key!

Chemistry

Chemistry is often thought of as the "middle ground" of the sciences: less memorisation than Biology and fewer equations and calculations than Physics. However, what it does hold in common with the other group 4 subjects is the focus during assessments on your understanding of the concepts.

There are a large number of concepts and processes - termed Understandings, Applications, and Skills by the IB - that you will be expected to have a firm grasp of by the end of your two years in the IB, and it can be difficult to a) make sense of all of them, and b) see how they are related. In addition to the usual benefits of listing what examiners expect you to know, the Chemistry syllabus is extremely useful. It is structured such that each topic is closely linked and dependent on the previous one: strong understanding in Atomic Structure allows easy rationalisation of Periodicity and Bonding; Bonding ties in to Energetics and from there to Kinetics, and then Equilibrium. Finally, Acids & Bases and Organic Chemistry rely on Equilibrium while Redox revisits material from Energetics. As such, while it may be tempting to consider revising for each topic as a stand-alone, constantly try to mentally link the concepts you see in each topic with ideas of the previous. This will help strengthen understandings of both topics, and also makes you less likely to be thrown by questions which skip between topics, which the papers like to do.

In relation to that, practice your past papers, and refer to their mark-schemes. Practicing the past papers allows you to become familiar with how questions are structured and get used to the thinking process required to answer the questions. It also highlights common pitfalls and mistakes that you may make while attempting the questions. The mark-schemes will also help you learn to keep focussed when answering the questions by understanding how marks are distributed: e.g. if a four-mark question asks for two solutions, chances are there's one mark for each answer and one for the reasoning of each. It is too easy to write down everything you can think of and lose precious time.

Finally, in line with this, understand what each question is asking for in the command terms (also in the syllabus). For example if they ask you to "state", you don't need to spend time on explaining how you know something; while if they ask you to "justify" you won't be able to get away with a one-word answer!

Environmental Systems and Societies

Environmental Systems and Societies (ESS) is one of the few IB interdisciplinary subjects, which means it meets the requirements of two different group subjects: 3 and 4. It is a great alternative for students who are not particularly confident in science, but it's still a demanding syllabus. It is therefore very important that ESS students have a good study plan for their exams, so we have some advice to help with revision.

Keep in touch with the environment

If you just stick to your textbook material, you are not learning the subject right. This applies to all subjects, but it seems particularly useful with ESS. In an age where environmental issues have become a massive concern, you should look to connect your studies to the real world. Read news, reports and articles related to the environment - climate change, pollution, habitat destruction and so on - and you will be able to give context to your knowledge. This is a very useful way to understand key syllabus concepts. Doing this also gives you facts for you to use in your Paper 2 essay-style questions, and increases your global awareness on issues that affect us as a society.

Use the IB official guide

The IB publishes a guide for each subject providing key information that you should take advantage of. Inside the guide you will find every sub-topic in the syllabus divided into three areas: significant ideas, knowledge and understanding, and applications and skills. Each point given under each area describes clearly and concisely what the IB wants you to learn and will assess you on. It is a good idea to study going through each point, as you will be assessed on these. Additional materials are always great to add depth to your studies and you should use them too, but your main starting point should be the IB guide.

Write review sheets after each topic

ESS topics are quite long, so you have to consolidate your learning as you go along. Every time you finish a topic, write a review sheet with the main things you've learned - it will help the information stick to you, plus you can use the sheet for further revision later on. If you find hard to remember the key facts, do your review sheet after every sub-topic or every couple of them.

Additionally, you can go further by making your own Quizlet or flashcards for each topic to quiz yourself. The important thing is to consolidate your learning and create your own review sheet/flashcards for when you need to do your final revision right before your exam.

Online revision

Sometimes, reading from notes is not enough, and you will need something else, such as a video. Revision videos are visually-appealing and can help information to stick to your brain. There are loads of ESS revision videos online, especially on YouTube, which you should have a look at. Don't aim to revise through the entire syllabus, at it would be a waste of time. Look for videos on topics or subtopics you aren't confident about to help you understand the key concepts and go on from there.

Apart from that, continue doing your revision as you would with other subjects - you should follow a revision technique that works for you and makes you feel comfortable with.

3.3.5 Group 5

Maths

When approaching Maths revision, for Studies, Standard, or Higher, the approach should be relatively similar. You must know the syllabus inside out, have attempted a very large number of past paper questions, and be very, *very* comfortable with your Graphing Calculator. Over the years, we've found that students often have weaknesses they've carried with them from earlier years (cross-multiplication for example) which they've found a workaround for. Address your weaknesses early, as these may prevent you from understanding more complex mathematical concepts later on. Sometimes, there is no substitute for doing 10 or 15 similar

questions in a row to really ingrain a concept in your brain.

When it comes to Maths, don't be afraid to be wrong. Some of the most elegant solutions come from attempting 3 or 4 different methods previously, only to realise where you've gone wrong. Get used to using scrap paper to attempt different 'routes' to a problem.

No two students are alike, and we can't assume to know where your strengths and weaknesses lie. However, if you put the effort in, you should see the rewards not only in your Maths results, but in your Science studies, Economics papers, and more. Focus on the fundamentals before difficult-sounding topics like Calculus & Statistics jump up on you, as being sure to build strong foundations ensures you can problem-solve with confidence when you come up against new and surprising questions.

During your studies/before your exam

- Know your formula booklet: It is incredible how many students approach their exams without knowing what every (or at least most) formulae in their booklets are used for, or what the variables stand for. These are gifts from the examiners, and especially for P1 where you won't have your calculator, it is the only familiar thing you'll have come exam time. Keep a copy at the front of your folder at all times, and annotate whenever you spot something of interest. For example, is $d(e^x)/dx$ *always* $= e^x$?
- Functions, functions, functions. If there is a common theme where students fall down, it is functions. Don't forget that calculus is, at its root, an extension of functions so if you don't understand functions inside out, you will be exposed in calculus questions. Work hard on understanding transformations, and being able to graph functions without a calculator, and without actual numbers. Can you graph $y = ax^2 - bx$?

Get used to writing clearly. There is a temptation in Maths to scrawl rapidly, but it is important to show your working neatly, to ensure you get the method marks in exams- tidy writing enables the examiner to follow your thought processes and more easily award you these marks.

During the exam

Read the question at least twice before starting to answer it. Particularly the seemingly easy questions will usually have a couple of buzz words in them that are effectively leading you towards the answer.

- If you can't figure something out, go straight to your formulae booklet, and on scrap paper just write down the formulae which might apply. You can then see if there is scope to manipulate them in some way to help answer your question. Sometimes, and particularly for trigonometry questions, trying a few different approaches to a question is often the right approach.
- Circle or underline how many marks are being awarded for each part of a question. if it says "write down" it means you should either already have the answer somewhere, or there should be a very quick step that you can take to get it. Try and spot any opportunities for this. Likewise if something is worth 6 marks and you only write down the answer, you won't get all the marks. Show all your working clearly and concisely.
- If the number you get for a final result (particularly on paper 1) isn't an integer or at least a fraction, there may be a mistake, so go back and cross check!
- Don't simplify anything to 3 significant figures as you do your working, only do this for your final result (and write 3SF alongside the result you are giving).
- For Paper 2, your calculator is your best friend and you should be trying to use it for every question. It won't always be required, but often trying to graph something and using different tools may help you get to your final solution.
- If you are feeling rushed for time, do the easy questions first, but on the longer questions, make sure you read the whole question. Often the hardest seeming ones actually have very

easy latter parts of the question, but because students get scared off, they leave it to last and rush through it.

- Last, but certainly not least, show your working.
- In fact, this is so important we're including it twice: *Show. Your. Working!*

Tutor Content

Tom is one of the most experienced and long-standing members of our team, and his wealth of experience goes a long way in developing teaching methods, keeping up to date with current trends in the IB, and knowing where the pitfalls lie for students. Not only this, but Tom also sat the IB himself, which places him in a unique place in being able to offer the top tips and strategies IB students need. He shared his experiences with us.

Tom became interested in becoming a tutor during Sixth Form when he "was often the person to go to for help with science homework," and making the natural progression whilst at university was a great way to share his knowledge and passion for science. These qualities are what made him stand out to EIB Education, as not only does he have a natural and amicable style, but his subject knowledge is second-to-none and continuing his studies in Mechanical Engineering at Imperial College London has only developed his passion for science.

"Most of the skills you need are already in your head, ready for the exam."

Attending a revision course is a "great way to consolidate the material that may have seemed very complex when covered in school," Tom told us, and he's "often heard from students that the courses gave them the confidence boost they needed to start the final push towards the exams." While he concedes that this is a very daunting time, "looking back, the skills of coursework juggling and time-pressured exam preparation have been invaluable at university."

To see it through Tom recommends that "the only way for students to make the process easier for themselves is to remain on-top of the workloads. Low confidence can make homework or coursework unnecessarily daunting, and asking for help is always more productive than worrying about not achieving your grades." Wise words!

Tom's lasting piece of advice is this;
"Believe it or not, you've already done the hard bit! Most of the skills you need are already in your head, ready for the exam. Nevertheless, the coming months are essential for you to hone your exam skills, and re-cover any patchy material. Two months of consistent work will ensure you achieve the grade you deserve!"

3.3.6 Group 6
Film Studies

Film is often overlooked as the 'easy' subject, one where you can get a grade by sitting around watching movies for 2 years. But anyone who has taken IB Film will know this is not true - in fact, it is actually a very demanding subject. You need to spend every single second of of a film paying attention to detail, thinking about the context, analysing the message and how it was sent. Then you have assessment that are really quite different from those of other subjects. So how can you tackle them?

External Assessment: Presentation
If you chose to study Film because you enjoy watching movies and wanted to explore them more deeply, this assessment will definitely be a fun one. When your teacher lists movies you can choose from, don't simply pick one you already enjoyed watching. You may not have the time to watch all of them, but at least watch 2 or 3 from the list. As you're watching keep some papers nearby and take brief notes on possible things you could explore, like themes, context, editing, *mise-en-scene*. Once you decide on a film, it is also a good idea to rewatch it again to list options for the 5 minute sequence rather than choosing the scene you remember most clearly.

During the presentation, explain your findings and analysis. Don't go too deep into the plot as the markers know what happens in the film. Focus instead on how the context shaped the film as well as how film language is used to convey a message.

External Assessment: Independent Study
Independent Study is a bit trickier - you have to choose your topic and films yourself. You want to keep in mind that you need films from different countries, so it is always best to keep the topic multicultural or multinational. Comparing styles or particular films from different cultures is a good start, or alternatively you can choose a more general theme apparent in film industries of different parts of the world MAYBE AN EXAMPLE WOULD BE HELPFUL HERE?. You might also want to keep in mind that you need to watch all of your chosen films, so it is a good idea to include some you watched already. Another good tip is to select films from a cultural context you know fairly well already.

Again, be careful not to centre your paper on the plots but focus instead on analysis and observations. Make sure it actually looks like a documentary script, and keep a balance on both visual and audio. Make use of the visual section to explain your analysis, rather than writing a whole essay in the audio section. Remember they are testing your knowledge on Film, so show how film can use both visuals and audio to tell a story.

Internal Assessment: Production Portfolio
If you decided to take Film because you just love making movies, this will definitely be the one for you. Except, you also need to make a portfolio explaining your procedures and outcomes, which may not be your thing. But it will not be difficult if you remember to keep track of everything. Jot down simple notes every time you do anything associated with the project, so that when you write your portfolio you'll have everything you need to write already.

The difficult part is making the film. You want to remember that you need to take every single step seriously. Brainstorm thoroughly before starting the script, and complete the best draft possible before moving on to shooting. Take every shot you want to take, and don't ever think you can "edit it out" to cover your mistakes. Leaving things for the next step will only lead to panic and regrets. Allow enough time for each process. An extra day in each step can help you think of a great idea to add to the film, write a brilliant scene, retake shots that are not good enough, and edit the film out to perfection.

Good point here, don't aim for perfection. Simply accept that we are still students and not professional filmmakers. Although we've been watching amazing films throughout the course, they can't be our standard. We can learn so much from them, but we need to use the resources and experiences *we* have. Aiming for perfection will only cause an immense amount of stress. Definitely try your best, but think of this film as a huge step in your filmmaking process, not the ultimate end project.

Studying Film is easy to enjoy if you simply like movies. The way you watch movies will change, and you might miss the old days when didn't have to think about every line, cut, music, or piece of item lying on the desk. But embrace the change and your deepened insight. Enjoy little details you weren't able to before, and embrace the little film critic and filmmaker within yourself.

3.4 Core

Theory of Knowledge (TOK)

Theory of Knowledge (TOK) is a unique component of the IB. It is like no other subject, making students think and reflect in ways they never have before, which might be why it manages to confuse so many students. One of the TOK assessment components is an externally-assessed essay. This essay can be quite tricky to master, but the following advice will hopefully help you get around it.

Break down the prescribed titles

You will start by choosing one of the six prescribed titles sent by the IB. Choosing the right title for you is vital, so take your time reading through them.

Break down each title: what is it asking for? Which Areas of Knowledge (AOKs) and Ways of Knowing (WOKs) do you have to use? Doing this will help you realise that maybe you have no idea about how to write a 1,600 word essay on the title you initially thought was perfect for you. Breaking down the title is a great way of knowing which title you can answer best, so make sure you take your time choosing.

Outline

As with all IB essays, you will need to do an outline to plan all your ideas. Once you've broken down your title, think about the Knowledge Questions (KQs) you want to address as well as the WOKs and AOKs you will address. From there, think about the arguments you want to make - this will help you identify your thesis and shape your body paragraphs. Make sure you think of counterarguments and limitations to your claims, as it is crucial that you provide these.

Evidence and own examples

Once you have your arguments, look for evidence if you don't have so already. Examples from your own life are a good starting point, but combine them with factual evidence, as you don't want to make generalisations based solely on your personal experiences. When selecting evidence, make sure you vary your sources: the news, the Internet, books, and so on. Make sure your evidence is relevant to your argument, and don't use cliches or overused examples - your examiner will be marking loads of essays, so if they see you're writing the same as everyone else, your essay will look weaker. Last but not least, as you find evidence you might find something that gives you a new claim or discredits the ones you already have... and that's alright! Keep an open mind and adapt your arguments to your findings, or use them as counterclaims.

Drafts

Drafts are vital in a TOK essay. You will not, I repeat, *will not*, get it right the first time. Finish your first draft ahead of time so you can leave it for a few days before going back to it. Seeing it with fresh eyes will let you see your weak points and come up with new ideas. Also, your teacher is only allowed to check your essay once, but that does not mean you cannot make all the drafts you need. You can even ask a friend or family member to read it and give you feedback, which will help you realise if all your arguments make sense and are clear to the reader.

TOK (Presentation)

TOK is difficult to get your head around. You find hard just learning about it, and now the IB wants you to *talk about it in front of your teacher and classmates*? Yes, the oral presentation is quite a daunting task to do, but it's worth a third of your TOK grade, so read on to find out how to ace your presentation and blow your peers' minds.

Your Real-Life Situation

For your presentation, you have to choose a real-life situation (RLS). This can be virtually anything as long as it is not a hypothetical scenario. It's in the name, really. Spend some time thinking about what you will talk about, as it will be the basis of your whole presentation. A personal example is a good option, but loads of people choose something they've seen on the news too. The important thing is that your RLS is simple and easy to explain - you don't want to lose your audience in a complex explanation of what your RLS really is.

You will then draft your Knowledge Question (KQ) from your RLS, which will inevitably influence which Areas of Knowledge (AOKs) and Ways of Knowing (WOKs) you choose. You can see your RLS is very important, but do not focus your presentation on

your RLS alone. Instead, focus on making links to your WOKs and AOKs and talk about the real TOK stuff, not your RLS.

Structure

Like in all presentations, your structure is key if you want your audience to understand what you are trying to say. Obviously, you need an introduction and a conclusion, but what about the main "body" of the presentation? Well, for each argument you make, follow this structure: **claim, counterclaim, mini-conclusion.** State your argument with its appropriate evidence, make a counter argument and point out implications, and wrap it up with a nice, brief conclusion. Do that for all your claims - you should have three separate ones. Your final conclusion at the end of your presentation should summarise all your arguments and reach a final answer on your KQ-- or as close to a 'final answer' as TOK can allow!

Terminology & Perspectives

Don't forget to use all the terminology from TOK. From WOKs to AOKs and everything in between. You will sound more professional and like you actually know what you are talking about (and hopefully you will do). When making claims, don't forget to mention different perspectives on the matter; how is your viewpoint different to someone of a different age, gender, cultural background, or ethnicity? Different perspectives not only make your presentation stronger, but will also let you identify limitations and implications of your claims and approach, which will help you think of counterclaims to include.

Presentation Style

Finally, there's no point in you making a great TOK presentation if your delivery makes the examiner fall asleep. You need to be an engaging speaker - change your tone, use rhetorical questions... You know, all those things TED Talk people do. Be careful with cue cards; if you start reading from them it may seem like you don't really know your material. If possible, do not have any notes with you and *never ever* look back and read from the slides. You should practise your presentation several times. **Good luck with your presentation!**

Extended Essay: General Advice

IB Diploma candidates have a lot on their plate. In addition to the rigorous study programme and TOK, you will also have to complete a 4,000 word research paper, the Extended Essay. It is an independent project where students have their advisers as their only official source of help, so it is normal to be unsure of how to craft the perfect Extended Essay. The truth is, there is not one single way to do it, but there are some things you could do to create the best paper you can.

The rubric

The most important thing is to understand what examiners want from you. Reading and understanding the grading criteria will be crucial for you to understand what you need to show and include in your 4,000 words. Your school should provide you with a copy, but you can also find the rubric online easily.

Exemplar essays

If you can, try to read through a couple of A-grade Extended Essays. You should pay attention to the content of these; how they analysed their evidence, how they structured their essay... But don't copy from them. Reading exemplar essays is about giving you an idea of what you have to do, not about letting you plagiarise someone else's work. There is no *one way* to make a good Extended Essay, so do not be afraid of being original and implementing your own ideas.

Research

Your research is the most important part of your essay, as the strength of your evidence will affect the quality of your arguments and analysis. Make sure you start early so you have time to research properly. Choosing a topic you are interested in is particularly important here, as you will have to spend long hours reading about it. There is no quick way to carry out your research; you may skim read and skip

sources at the expense of missing out on very important information for your essay.

Outlines and drafts

Your essay structure is extremely important, so you have to get it perfect. The only way to do this is to outline your essay carefully before you start. Otherwise, your essay will be all over the place. Moreover, you will need to write several drafts - at least two is recommended. Your first draft may look great, but read it over a couple of days later and you will find there is room for improvement. Doing a few drafts will ensure your essay is as good as you can make it.

Word count

Be very careful with your word count, as you cannot go over the limit. Ideally, you should try to get as close to 4,000 words as possible because it will allow you to write a more in-depth essay. At the same time, do not try to force getting to the limit. Remember, it is quality over quantity, so if you think your essay says it all at 3,800 words, do not try to stick 200 words just to fill in. Make sure you check what is included in the word count and what is not, as you do not want to be penalised for accidentally going over the limit.

References

The worst thing that could happen to you is to fail your Extended Essay because of unintentional plagiarism. You do not want all your hard work to go to waste like that, so make sure that you cite and reference everything you take from another source. Even if you are paraphrasing or taking a general idea, make sure you reference your source in text and in your bibliography. Also, do not leave your references until you finish writing your essay. Do them as you write your body so that you save time later on and so that you do not forget to cite anything. Remember to find the most appropriate referencing format for your discipline, and stick to only one format throughout- this oughtn't need saying but unfortunately student have opted to switch referencing styles half-way through writing their EE and then never get round to changing the first few references to the new style!

Although challenging, your Extended Essay will hopefully be an interesting experience too. Make sure you start your essay in advance, so if you encounter any problems you will have time to overcome them and produce a great research paper.

Extended Essay: Choosing A Topic & Question

When beginning thinking about their Extended Essay, many students feel the required length is just way too long - what can you actually write about for 4,000 words? What if your topic or question wasn't suitable, and you only realised after 3,900 words? How will you know if the topic is right for you? How do you even find one in the first place?

First, start by choosing your subject. Don't simply go with your favourite one. Keep several in mind and brainstorm different topics you can go into for each. Once you have explored both subject and topic choices deeply enough, you will get a sense of which one works best. Extended Essay guidelines vary between different subjects, so make sure to read them thoroughly before deciding on a subject. It is highly advisable to choose one that is taught at your school, so a teacher will be there for you when you have questions. It will also make it easier to choose a subject you study, as you'll acquire sufficient knowledge in the area while also making sure your Extended Essay does not overlap with the syllabus.

When choosing the topic, make sure it's interesting enough to engage you. You want to conduct your own research and form your own analysis. You will want a topic that you can develop strong opinions on and can find enough resources to analyse and discuss. Be original and creative - don't choose something that's been discussed by many academics already. Try to find your own area where you can make your own discoveries and findings.

Formulating a question is the next step, and a difficult one. You want a question that invites views from different perspectives as well as a thorough analysis and criticism. You want something with context you can go into, and it can't have an obvious answer with no need for any research. You want the question to be able to summarise your essay while also serving as a very brief introduction, as you don't want it to be too wordy or extensive.

There is no guidance on *what* you should choose as your topic and question, because it all depends on your own interests and ideas. The only advice is to be independent in your choices - don't simply choose one because it seems easy and everyone seems to be doing it. The topics that interest you will be the easiest for *you*. So take time to brainstorm and explore different ideas. Don't rush - 4,000 words sound like a lot, but they don't actually take that long to write. You will have enough time to think and explore deeply before writing your first sentence.

3.5 General Advice

3.5.1 Using past papers

At the core of the IB's ethos is a move away from exam-focused syllabus. There are only one set of exams at the end rather than throughout the programme, most subjects have a large portion of Internal Assessment as part of the examined grade (usually 20%+), and the exam styles are constantly changing to ensure students can't succeed by rote learning.

With that said, understanding, disseminating, and painstakingly reviewing past papers is par for the course, both for the IB and the majority of school leaving programmes.

A few things to be aware of:
Most IB syllabi change every 3-8 years, so it is your responsibility if reviewing historical past papers that you know if questions asked are relevant to the current syllabus.

- If you are struggling to find past papers for a given subject as the syllabus only changed recently, do seek out specimen papers, which your teachers should be able to provide, as these provide a good insight into how the questions are likely to be phrased and structured.
- The IB has 2 exam sessions, in May and November each year, roughly correlating to the Northern and Southern Hemispheres. Within these two sessions, there are usually two time zones (shown as TZ1 and TZ2 on exam papers). This means in any one year, you will have up to 4 sets of past papers per subject to get your teeth stuck into, although do be aware that some subjects are only examined in one session (May or November) each year, so check this before you race through all the available papers!
- The very worst habit you can form is doing a past paper with the mark scheme to hand. You should try your best to attempt a question multiple times before resorting to the mark-scheme, as tempting as it might be. Once you have reviewed the mark-scheme, go back and answer the question (in full) without it.
- As you go through your IB, try to regularly attempt past paper questions. It will give you insights into exam strategy, wording of IB style exam questions, and allocation of marks.
- In most papers, you can see at the front how many marks the paper is comprised of (for example, 120). If you know it is a 2 hour exam then you know roughly how many minutes you should be spending per mark (2-hours = 120 minutes / 120 marks = 1 minute per mark)

- Get used to attempting past papers in a timed environment, and ideally away from the comfort of your bedroom, to try to replicate exam conditions -- maybe even frequent your school or local library, or ask a teacher to use their classroom!
- Different subjects require different approaches to the use of past papers. While you may be able to work through several papers a day for Maths and Sciences once you get into the rhythm of attempting them, there is no sense in being quite as strict with any essay-based subjects (e.g. Language A and many Group 3 subjects). As you approach your exams, you simply do not have time to write practice essays for every single question that has ever come up; while it is certainly important to write timed essays for practice, the most efficient revision strategy is to make essay plans for as many questions as you can, in order to get accustomed to the process of generating ideas and developing a structure quickly in response to a prompt. Follow up by attempting timed essays for a small selection of these plans to ensure you have all bases covered.

Final Advice
- We are inclined to say you *shouldn't* attempt last year's past papers until close to your final exams. It is the closest example you will have to the real thing and is great practice material as close to the final exam date as possible.
- Be strict with yourself when attempting past papers: better to make silly mistakes now (and thus learn from them) than in the real exams!

5.5.2 Choosing your subjects
Undoubtedly the most important step in your IB journey, but don't be phased by this. A few pointers to take on board before making your final decision:

Do your research
Speak to classmates in the year above to find out how they've managed with certain subjects. Is HL Chemistry really as difficult as people make it out to be? Are there great subject combinations which

work well together, such as Economics & Business Management, Maths & Physics, or History & Literature?

Speak to your teachers

If you are lucky enough to have taken the MYP, you will have a good sense for the kind of content taught in the different subjects you're taking, so speak to your MYP teachers about how they feel you've performed in certain subjects. Otherwise, get hold of the subject briefs for the IB subjects you are considering and compare these with your current studies, preferably with your and your future IB teachers so they can help you determine what skills you already have.

Look ahead

If you've started to consider your university options, it is worth looking at whether the courses or universities you're considering ask for certain subjects, or even certain scores. Did you know that the London School of Economics in London asks for a 7 at HL Maths to study Economics, for example, or that the University of Edinburgh require a 5 in SL English for any subject, regardless of its literary content (or lack of!)? Spend some time talking to your parents and friends about which university subjects you might want to study, and look at which subject combinations might work, but in terms of best preparing you, and also which subject combinations they might ask for.

Have a rough point tally in mind

If you think you're targeting 36 points from your IBDP, try to break this down into its component parts. What do you think you would get for Maths Studies? Theatre? Add up your scores, perhaps introducing a one point buffer either side, to see what your expected maximum and minimum score might be. It might shed some light on certain subjects which you should reconsider taking.

HL vs. SL?

The IB suggests 150 hours for SL subjects and 240 hours for HL. Of course, the differences are often more nuanced than that, but this should give you an indication of the teaching time, and your studying time. Remember that universities will predominantly look at your HL subjects, so make sure they fit with your desired career choice, although your SLs will contribute up to half of your academic points, so do not neglect these!. Pick 3 HLs you're definitely going to enjoy studying, and grant yourself a bit more flexibility with your SLs, hopefully also to enjoy but possibly to try something you haven't studied before, or for 'easier' points.

It **isn't** impossible to change your SLs and HLs once you've started – if your school permits it – but it is very difficult to entirely switch subjects. If, once you've started, you realise that you've made a mistake, be sure to address it in your first term. You can play catch up over the first extended break.

Have a theme

It isn't necessary to be a 'science' student or an 'arts' student to succeed in the IB. Some of the best students will pick 6 subjects which don't naturally fit together with any common thread. With that said, it is in your interests to have a general theme to your studies, as this will help to guide your methods of working and studying.

Make it personal

Finally, it has to be a personal choice, not your parents' or your school's. If you've followed the advice above, you should be giving yourself a great chance of succeeding.

Fundamentally, try to select subjects **you both enjoy, and are good at.** Don't only pick subjects which you deem easy, as chances are you will either fall out of love with the subject early on and perform poorly, or feel disengaged due to not being stretched academically in your areas of interest.

Remember that you are lucky to still study six subjects in your final two years of school, where many state curricula mean you will only be studying three or four. Embrace the opportunities this affords you, do your research and have fun.

Exemplar subject combinations:

The Medic
Careers like: Doctor or Clinical Researcher

HL: Biology, Chemistry, Maths
SL: English Literature, German B, History

The Artist
Careers like: Sculptor or Curator

HL: Visual Art, Literature & Performance, Anthropology/Art History
SL: Italian *ab initio*, ESS, Maths (Studies)

The Linguist
Careers like: Film Translator or Ambassador

HL: French B, Spanish B, English Language & Literature
SL: Psychology, Biology, Maths

The Economist
Careers like: Stock Broker or Data Scientist

HL: Economics, Business Management, Maths
SL: English Language & Literature, Physics, French *ab initio*

The Engineer
Careers like: Formula One or Civil Engineer

HL: Maths, Physics, Computer Science
SL: English Literature, Economics, German

The Social Scientist
Careers like: Disaster Analyst or Cartographer

HL: History, Geography, ESS
SL: Maths, English Language & Literature, Mandarin

The Architect
Careers like: Urban Planner or Surveyor

HL: Visual Arts, Maths, Physics
SL: French, English Literature, Art History

The All-Rounder
Careers like: Inventor or Historian

HL: Chemistry, History, English Literature
SL: Latin, Maths, Biology

5.5.3 Working smart, not hard

One of the keys to successfully enjoying the IB and translating this enjoyment into exam success is to understand *how* what you learn in the classroom will be assessed, and *how to show* that you not only understand the basics, but are comfortable with the more advanced aspects of each subject. Exam papers provide the opportunity to do this, as does each piece of internally assessed work, but students need to know *how* to show their knowledge, and not rely on simply having learnt it.

We recommend familiarising yourself with the syllabus and previous exam papers of each subject you take, as well as reading through the exemplar pieces of coursework on the IBO website before handing in any IA or other assessed work. Each piece of work should carry a piece of you through it, in terms of your lexis, methods of expression, and most of all, interest *in* and individual perspective *on* the subject area, but you also need to learn how to shout to your examiners that you are demonstrating each key attribute in your subjects. The IB is hard work, but those who achieve the top grades often find that understanding what was required reduced wasted time, and allowed them to focus throughout their studies and revise more efficiently when the time came. Oh, and make great notes from the very beginning- there is nothing more frustrating than trying to revise from half a crumpled side of A4 covered in indecipherable scrawls!

3.6 Internal Assessments (IAs)

3.6.1 General advice

Up to half of humanities subjects, such as languages, can be examined as Internal Assessments. That means up to *12 of the 42 points available in your 6 subjects can be moderated as IAs.* **Treat your IAs as exams, and not as homework.** If you handle your IAs well, you could be in a situation where you can sit down for an exam knowing you only need a strong 5 in your exams to get a 7 overall.

Draft, draft, and draft again. Do not procrastinate. The key to getting consistently good marks in IAs across your subjects is to put each task in perspective. When completing an assignment, you spend roughly half of your time producing 90% of the work, and another half on that last 10%. Do not agonise over every detail or become overwhelmed by the task as a whole, but start with a plan and work up.

For each piece of work, it is vital to contextualise what needs doing, and to begin with a plan, in order to make best use of your time- write a plan, roughly structured into introduction, middle/research and conclusion, for each project as you receive the assignment, in order to have an overview of the work required.

Begin to flesh this out into full sentences by jotting down your ideas as you research. Do not worry about wording or proof-reading at this stage. You can leave the full writing of your introduction and conclusion until the end, so long as your ideas are all in one place and you have a clear structure as above.

From here, you have your first draft. Read over your research to decide on your argument. You can now write out your essay by turning your notes into full sentences with analysis and an argument to follow.

Proof-read the final draft and pare down the word count if necessary. It is always better to have to cut words than to be struggling to hit word count! Remember, though, clarity is key. When cutting down your essay, make sure that the argument remains clear; you will get more marks for an essay that answers the question and is easy to follow than for a convoluted argument. If you struggle with this, try to reduce each paragraph to the key points, and ask yourself 'What is each sentence adding to my analysis?'

Finally, do not submit anything without checking what you have written against the mark-scheme and assessment criteria for this piece of work- ensure you have used specific terminology and included all required sections, to make it easy as possible for the Examiners to award you marks.

5.5.2 Subject-specific advice
Group 1 - Language A - Language & Literature

The IB Language & Literature course is a real opportunity for you to explore a variety of different text types, and the written tasks reflect that. The written task 1, taken at both HL and SL, is a chance for you to try writing in a non-academic style - probably a welcome break for everyone! Students are required to complete a written task from the literary part of the course, and one from the language part of the course.

As usual, choosing your topic might be the most daunting stage of the process. Luckily, you can make it easy for yourself - which part of the texts studied in class did you particularly like? Was there a character from a literary work that you would enjoy imagining in a totally different setting, and writing about their thoughts? Were you frustrated with the final chapter of a work such that you are determined to re-script an alternative ending? Or, for the language part of a course, how would you feel about putting yourself in a journalist's shoes and responding to a speech or advertisement you have studied? This is a chance for you to get creative with your literary texts. Don't write an essay; pick something relevant to the course (check with your teacher if you're unsure); and demonstrate a clear knowledge of the conventions of your chosen text type.

The second written task, for HL students only, is a critical response to one of 6 prescribed questions. Your response is this time an essay, and should critically analyse your chosen text to provide a comprehensive and analytical response to the question. Again, try and make your life easier by picking a text that you will find straightforward and quick to analyse. The IB will not discriminate against students who picked 'easier' texts, as long as your response is excellent. Hence, there is no point choosing to analyse Tolstoi unless you have a very good reason to do so - you can very easily choose to analyse a comic book you read and critically analyse how it would be received by different people at different times, and why. The Language & Literature course is one of the IB courses that gives you the most freedom in terms of your IAs: don't be scared to get creative!

Oral Component

The oral components of this course consist of an Individual Oral Commentary (IOC) and Further Oral Activity (FOA). The IOC is a literary commentary on an extract chosen by the examiner from the works studied in class. Make sure you know the extracts back to front and choose some literary tools that you will be confident analysing on the day, and relate them to the two guiding questions received. Think about how these shape the text's meaning and influence your feelings as a reader. Why did the writer choose to say that in that way? What could they have said instead and why did they choose not to? How might context shape these choices? You should go into the exam with a relatively good idea of what you are going to say for each possible extract. Your prep time should be spent jotting down all of these prepared ideas, so you don't forget them when you start talking, and making sure your structure is clear. Bring in highlighters and pens and annotate just as you would normally, and practice sections of the oral if you feel that might help you. Walking into the exam after the prep, remember that you have practiced these before and that you just need to do the same thing again - it will be over in no time.

The Further Oral Activity

This oral is much less formal, and not recorded for moderation. You also several chances and can pick your best grade, so there is less pressure than the IOC. You're also allowed to present as a group. This is probably not the easiest way of doing things, as each student has to contribute significantly and is graded individually - you will not be rewarded for the work of your peers. You also have less control over what you do, so unless you have a really good reason for working in a group it is probably best to avoid doing so. As always, pick a subject you find particularly interesting and, hopefully, easier to analyse. Make sure you have a good visual presentation to keep people engaged, don't read off your notes, and make eye contact with the people in front of you. A good tip for making a presentation

engaging is varying the tone of your voice - monotony is not exciting for anyone!

Language A – Literature

The Literature course is probably one of the IB's most creative academic subjects. It is concerned with the analysis of how people's stories and emotions are presented in works of literature from around the world. Key to the course is how context shapes literature, so keep that in mind as you brainstorm your topic for your written task, and throughout your writing; examiners want to see that you can seamlessly link the content of the story to the context in which it was set and written. Think about how a translated work might differ from the original and how that might have influenced what you read. The written assignment, based on a work in translation, should be seen as a journey from the first step of the class discussion to the final essay. You should base your topic on the subjects touched upon in the discussion, as well as your supervised writing exercise, but the IB is not prescriptive here - so definitely take the time to consider what aspect of the work you would most enjoy working on. Make sure that you can realistically tackle your question within the set word limit, so don't choose something too broad, as that will hinder your ability to undertake a rigorous analysis, but also keep in mind that you have quite a lot of freedom to interpret your question in a way that suits what you want to do. Make the most of this opportunity to let your personal take on the works come through!

Oral Component

The Individual Oral Commentary is an oral analysis of one of the texts studied in class. At HL, it is followed by a discussion of another work studied. Your advantage for this exam is that you know your texts before the oral, even if you don't know exactly which passage is going to come up. Be clever, re-read them the day before, and think of pre-prepared structures of answers you can deliver on, which are flexible to change depending on the text. Identify the key themes, and accompanying literary techniques. Why did the writer choose to use that turn of phrase, and not another? What are they trying to express, and why? What effect does this have on the reader? Before the actual exam, do something completely different to get your mind off the upcoming challenge. Approach the preparation time in a way that suits you. That might include scrawling all over the text, or rehearsing a structure to yourself. You should be able to quickly gather your thoughts before entering the exam, so don't rush yourself, and you will be fine!

Group 2

In IB Language B, you have probably been able to practice reading and writing almost every class. But this time, the internal assessment wants you to speak, which you may have not been able to practice as often. So here are some tips on acing your IA, which can be very stressful if you don't speak the language regularly.

The first and most important thing is to be comfortable speaking the language. This rarely happens overnight, so you will probably need to practice speaking frequently. This can be difficult if you don't live in the country where the language is spoken. If this is the case, make the most out of your class time. Practice talking with your teacher and other students because after all, they are the best people to practice with - you will be assessed speaking with them, not anyone else.

If you are lucky enough to find other people speaking the language, you can use that opportunity to your advantage as well. Meet them as often as possible and try to speak your Language B rather than an easier one you speak every day. If that is not the case, but you feel like practice outside of class is needed, try finding movies or TV shows in the language. Use your free time you would have spent watching movies and TV shows anyway. If you don't enjoy watching stuff, you can listen to songs instead. Find something you enjoy doing, so you will find yourself doing it regularly.

Most importantly, try to relax and think of the assessment as simply having regular conversations, just in another language - which can be very difficult

and stressful, but not that different from what we do every day anyway.

Group 3

This Group consists of subjects like Business Management, History, Information Technology in a Global Society (ITGS), and Philosophy. Here we've chosen to focus on Economics.

It can feel daunting when you have to write not one but three Economics IAs. How do you find the time to write all of them, when you struggle to write even one for some subjects? The good news is, Economics IAs are really not a struggle as long as you find something interesting to write about.

Start by finding a news article. It is important to find one not focused on economics, as you want to do the analysis yourself. Feel free to find an article completely irrelevant, as long as it has some elements you can draw from to explain IB Economics knowledge. Browse through news websites to find your options, and it is a good idea to keep several open to explore potential topics and materials for each.

An easy way to do this is by starting an IA for each topic as you just finish learning the topic in class. You will have a clear understanding of materials in the topic while they are still fresh in your memory. It will also help you prevent cramming three IAs in a week.

You can also make the whole process more interesting by finding articles of your interest. It could be about anything from robots to environmental issues. You could also find articles from different countries, as many newsagents around the world now have articles written in English. This will deepen your analysis as you will be able to explore economics of different countries associated.

Just by reading an article you may have a vague idea on what to write about, but it might not be enough to cover a whole IA. Simply look over your notes or textbook to make a rough guide on all materials covered in the topic. Make particular note of specific economics terms and graphs that you can incorporate into your IA. You can then start writing out an outline, linking class material to specific details in your article.

As a final step, make the most out of your teacher's comments to create the best final draft possible. Try to create a good draft before handing it in so your teacher does not need to comment on simple mistakes, and can focus on real advice instead. Take every single piece of advice into account when writing your final draft, making sure it acknowledges all the requirements by the IB as well as your teacher.

Economics IA can be enjoyable if you find something you like to write about. Explore different articles and ideas to find ones that work best for you.

Group 4

Group 4 consists of the Sciences students can study on the IB. Here we've chosen to focus on Biology.

If you have always dreamt of being a scientist, here's your chance to shine. If you've never been interested in becoming a scientist, here's an opportunity to try it out. Science may not be for everyone - but investigations can be, if you just find something interesting to explore.

The first step is finding a topic. I'm sure you have lots of interests, so try to think like a scientist and one that can be approached with biology. In fact, Biology, like most sciences, is literally everywhere, so it won't be too difficult. The only thing you want to be cautious about is finding a topic explored by too many students or a topic that leads to a way too simple investigation that it hardly amounts to an IB internal assessment. Try to avoid these issues and find something you genuinely want to investigate scientifically. Be original and creative; try to find something unique that no one has explored before. Then plan your investigation like a scientist too. Think of equipment you will need and how you will get them if you don't have them at home. Your school

may be willing to lend you some or you might have to spend extra time at school to finish your investigation.

An important thing to remember is how we're not actually scientists, despite our efforts to think and plan like them. Accept that you will make mistakes, and that even scientist make mistakes. Plan out enough time for your investigation so you can afford to give several tries. Calculate your error and think what factors may have caused even greater errors. Don't try to cover up your mistakes but reflect on them. Think about what the results actually mean and try to explain them scientifically. Focus more on your discoveries rather than mere descriptions of what happened. Use the scientific knowledge you already have or even go through further research. Try to engage scientific terms - write like a scientist too. Don't get too caught up with descriptive language and merely serve the purpose of describing what happened.

Your Biology internal assessment will be very scientific and professional, but there's no need to be scared. It simply means you will view things and describe them from a scientific perspective. It can be a fun opportunity to explore your interests in a new way. Have fun and explore the world of biology like you never have before.

Group 5

For your Mathematics SL IA, you have to do what the IB calls the Mathematical Exploration. This is a piece of written work that involves investigating an area of mathematics. It is graded out of 20 marks in total and contributes to 20% of your total grade, so it is worth doing well in it, especially if you are aiming for a 6 or a 7. There are some things you need to keep in mind if you want to create a great IA.

Personal engagement

4 of your total 20 marks are just for showing personal engagement, so aim to get these easy marks. Yes, you can show personal engagement by choosing a topic you are interested in, but you should show it throughout your entire IA. Write in the first person, present the maths in your own style, talk about how you felt (yes, don't be shy to say you were surprised or frustrated) as your investigation moved forward, and so on.

Structure and presentation

How clearly and well you present your work is worth around 7 marks (4 for communication and 3 for your mathematical presentation). Thus, make sure you have a proper structure and your vocabulary and notations are flawless. They are easy points to get, as long as you pay attention to detail, so take your time to edit your work.

It's okay to be wrong

If your exploration goes wrong at any point, use it to your advantage. If you prove yourself wrong, or find that what you found was not what you were hoping for, write it down and make it clear. Point out the flaws during your investigation as well as what went well. If you do this throughout your body, you will be showing that you are reflecting on your work, which is another 3 easy marks to get. Recognising your errors can give you the extra marks you need to reach your desired grade.

Keep it simple

Most students go crazy trying to use complex mathematics to impress their teachers. In reality, you only need to use a level of maths equivalent to the SL syllabus. The IB is more concerned about how you show your knowledge and understanding of the mathematical topic you choose. So, make sure you choose something hard enough for Maths SL, but something you understand well and can prove you are knowledgeable of. It's better to keep it simple and do that than overcomplicating your investigation and end up confused and not knowing what you are saying. If you don't leave it until the last minute, your IA will surely go well.

Group 6

This group of subjects on the IB consists of the Arts subjects students can pursue, including Dance, Music, Theatre and Visual Arts. Here we've chosen to focus on Film.

IB Film has a relatively big internal assessment. Not only do you have to create a whole film but you also have to write an extensive portfolio explaining everything. It is a long process but something you will enjoy doing, especially if you chose IB Film in the first place.

Before you start anything, watch movies for inspirations. If you don't have enough time to spend hours watching even more films, you can simply think about ones you really enjoyed or thought were well made. Rather than focusing on their plot twists and character developments (which are still helpful for writing a screenplay), analyse the film language for inspirations on how to *film*. Look through different shots and edits as well as the role music plays and how the film sets its own mood. Don't try to copy them but extract ideas to create your own. Remember to take note of these films; they will be excellent to mention in your portfolio.

Once you start planning, give each stage enough time - especially editing. Making 'perfect' edits is impossible, but every time you rewatch your film you will be able to spot more and more edits you want to make. The only thing stopping you will be time. So make sure to leave several days to edit. After a good night's sleep your film will look different and you may be able to find even more ideas for edits.

I cannot stress enough how important it is to take each step seriously. It is very tempting to leave work for the next step so your current work will be easier and quicker. You might decide to leave your screenplay as it is because your actors can have spontaneous dialogues to fill the scene. Or you may shoot only one take because you can simply edit it to make it better. This is the worst mistake you can make. Always remember that when rubbish goes in, rubbish comes out. If you make sure every step is done at its best, it will make the next step so much easier and your end product so much better.

When you start writing your portfolio journal, try to incorporate every material you learned in class. Look over class notes and use specific film words you learned to explain various styles of shots and edits. Reference filmmakers and particular films as inspirations. Explain your process but include reflection wherever you can, to focus on what you've learned rather than what you've done.

Creating a film feels like a lot of pressure. But rather than an assessment, think of it as a project you always wanted to try. You love movies, now you simply get to make your own!

3.7 Extended Essays (EEs)

The crucial requirement for your EE is that it must fit the guidelines of a subject offered in the IBDP programme. As you will need a supervisor to guide you, it is highly recommended that you first choose a subject from those taught at your school, or that you have specific subject areas for a World Studies EE and a teacher with expertise in at least one of these areas.

As a note, the World Studies EE is not offered by all schools, but is growing in popularity as more and more students embrace the interdisciplinary aspect of the course- indeed, in the most recent May statistical bulletin, World Studies was the 7th most popular subject for EEs across the global cohort. Students must focus on a global issue of significance, and examine it across multiple disciplines, presenting tightly-focused local research and suggestions, and linking this to the global impact of this issue. It is a difficult subject to take your EE in, but many students who engage fully with it find it a valuable and fascinating challenge.

After selecting your area and confirming your supervisor, you can narrow down your ideas, following your interests to choose a topic. You will be most successful choosing a topic you are interested in, as after all, you will have to spend lots of time researching this area! However, it is essential to know the guidelines before you embark on research. For example, in Economics, you may be interested in answering a theoretical question along the lines of assessing the influence of Keynes in modern economic thought, as this was the most interesting part of your Economic course to you. A topic such as this, however, is not suitable for an Economics EE, as you are required to carry out a specific investigation, including your own data collection, and this essay title is too general and difficult to research in a comprehensive and relevant fashion. For all subjects, you will be unable to read all previous research and criticism of your preferred wide subject area, making a generalised or 'story-telling' question unsuitable for the Extended Essay. Make sure you understand the actual requirements of your preferred subject, and are not just being seduced by a 'Big Idea'- narrow it down to your precise area of interest, and not only will you produce a better EE, but we think you will enjoy writing it more too!

Make sure your essay flows. This can be achieved by breaking it into smaller 'chapters' when you are writing, and focusing on making each chapter link to one another. This ensures that your essay is successful as a whole, and does not fall into the doldrums in the middle- which is surprisingly common. Try reading your first full draft using only the first and last sentences of each paragraph. Do you still have a logical argument? If not, your essay may not be flowing intuitively.

Finally, there are many IB students who have great ideas and research for their Extended Essays, but fail to achieve the top marks because of their formatting or layout. Examiners want to give you as many marks as possible, so ensure you not only write to the subject requirements of your EE, but also include a title page, footnotes/references, bibliography, and all other small 'non-academic' aspects of the work.

3.7 Theory of Knowledge (TOK)

Theory of Knowledge, or TOK, divides IB students, but it is almost universally looked back on with immense fondness by IB graduates, as it provides a truly unique outlook on learning as part of a holistic educational programme. We strongly recommend students think carefully about their presentation topic, as unlike the Extended Essay, simply being interested in an area and willing to research it extensively does not mean it has sufficient potential for TOK exploration. However, with a good understanding of the key requirements for TOK, of the meaning of the *Areas of Knowledge* and *ways of knowing*, and what constitutes a Knowledge Question, students can apply many aspects of their personal, moral, and academic interests to their TOK presentation.

When it comes to the TOK essay, be sure to plan your answer with on eye on the assessment criteria; too many students are overwhelmed by the admittedly vague essay titles and fail to remember this is an assessed essay like any other. The basics do not change- plan your answer, draft and re-draft, leave time for editing, and be sure you have answered the question to the best of your ability, no matter how odd the prompt!

3.8 CAS: Making the most of your summer

CAS may seem like a slightly daunting task, or a secondary concern to the academic aspects of the Diploma, however it is a great opportunity to take a break from your studies, engage in some other activities, and also complement your learning through developing essential skills.

We spoke to two of our excellent tutors who are recent IB graduates, Dara and Sophie, about how they fulfilled their CAS requirements and what the benefits of this core element of the IBDP are.

Fulfilling each requirement might seem like a chore, but don't forget that you don't necessarily have to do something new- you can continue with old projects or activities and look to extend your skills in these areas. As Dara explained, she did a mixture of new and old activities.

"For Creativity, I took piano lessons for the entirety of DP1 & DP2 – this was not a new activity, but rather one I was continuing with. My Activity component included kickboxing, basketball, a Via Ferrata school trip we did in DP1, as well as obtaining my "Sports Leaders UK" certification, which then meant I could lead sports classes and PE lessons and help organise sports days for younger students… I also worked with Amnesty international, and as a head of my school's Dance Committee."

Similarly Sophie continued with activities that she already enjoyed, football and swimming, while taking the opportunity to explore new skills through taking art classes. Sophie also volunteered at a retirement home and "conducted a lot of fundraising events to fund my trip with Operation Wallacea over summer, which counted towards the different categories of CAS as well." Through Operation Wallacea, Sophie participated in a conservation research project, building further skills which she has been able to put to use strengthening her university applications and during her undergraduate studies.

Completing these activities were not only necessary to receive the Diploma, as Sophie told us, "CAS ensures that students still continue to lead a balanced life." Through completing CAS, Dara "learned a lot about... how I work with others, deal with stress, and manage my time". It is these additional skill and experiences that make the CAS such an integral part of the Diploma Programme, assisting students to "help build and strengthen other personality traits and qualities, such as teamwork, cooperation or international mindedness, all of which also tie in heavily with the aims of the IB", Dara added.

Although the projects you undertake may be a struggle at times, especially during busy times of the Diploma Programme, the heavy workload does have a value and outcome. Sophie explained that; "I think attending and fundraising for the trip with Operation Wallacea to Sulawesi, Indonesia... allowed me to experience things that I had never done before, which helped me grow as a person and gave me a lot of self-confidence, which supported me throughout my last year of IB."

Dara was also able to utilise the difficult times to build and grow as an individual and a student of the IB, "learning to get through those struggles really emphasised the importance of putting my own desires to one side, and focusing on what I had to do."

Beyond this, CAS also has great benefits when making your university applications. Dara explained that:

"When I was applying for Economics, I spoke of how I had been able to apply my theoretical understanding of Economics to the the real-life situation of managing a budget and setting suitable prices whilst being a part of my school's Dance Committee. Even

though most of my CAS activities were irrelevant to my application, I strongly believe that they are still very useful for university, either for my fitness, social awareness, or time-management."

In order to make the most of your CAS experiences, both Dara and Sophie recommend doing things that you enjoy, in order to ensure you are getting the most out of the time to plan ahead and set yourself clear goals. These skills are not only essential for CAS, but will help you in your studies at Diploma level and beyond.

So, don't think of CAS as merely another tick-boxing exercise. You should have fun, build on your current skills and successes, and take the opportunity to challenge yourself to build new skills that will be beneficial to your studies and help ensure you graduate from the IB as a well-rounded individual.

3.9 Memorisation Techniques

After almost two years of learning, there will inevitably be a significant amount of content to memorise in preparation for your final exams. While some subjects are more systematic than others and place a greater emphasis on knowledge application (e.g. Maths, Physics, Chemistry), all require some degree of memorisation. In fact, the sheer volume of content covered in certain subjects can feel overwhelming, but there are a number of techniques you can employ to reduce the stress involved and make the whole process a little more manageable.

Firstly, make sure you are not memorising more than you need to. This is where your syllabus becomes especially important: remove any superfluous information from your notes to ensure they are streamlined, exam-focused and, ultimately, easier to memorise!

Unless you have a truly excellent (perhaps even photographic) memory, you are unlikely to find that the notes you have made in class provide the best basis for revision. As such, you will probably need to reformulate them in a form to suit you (more on this below), which also provides a great opportunity to supplement any gaps in your knowledge with information from textbooks, online resources, and any other support you may be receiving.

Here are some great ways to help with memorisation:

- Mind maps can be an excellent way of summarising large volumes of information in a condensed, visually appealing form. They take a little time to get used to as you may have to work hard to re-organise your notes at first (so do find a tutorial online as a guide!), but they can provide a very intuitive means of visually arranging material and demonstrating connections between concepts.
- Flashcards are a useful on-the-spot means of testing specific knowledge- perhaps a definition or other short answer. Use past papers to establish the sort of questions you could be asked, and turn these into a set of flashcards for each sub(-topic). There are also plenty of apps and pieces of software out there to help you make these if you would prefer to have them in a digital format, and this also means you can revise wherever you are!
- Memory palaces (also known as 'memory journeys' or 'the method of loci') are an innovative way of solidifying knowledge, attaching facts, objects or concepts to your spatial memory so that they can be more easily accessed on recall. You begin by imagining a place such as a house or palace, then define a route within this space, and finally associate the information you want to remember with given storage points along the way. The more creative (or even absurd) you are with the images you form within this route, the more memorable the information will be. As a technique, it does admittedly require some practice (and online tutorials will again be helpful here), but can be an excellent long-term memory strategy if you find it suits the way your mind works. For 'research' here, see the BBC's *Sherlock*, where the titular detective utilises his 'mind palace' to great dramatic effect.

Importantly, remember that everyone learns and memorises in a different way, so if you find that it works best for you simply to write information down over and over again (i.e. 'motor reproduction'), that is absolutely fine! It is certainly worth experimenting with a variety of different techniques while revising throughout your time in the IB, so that you have ideally established your preferences before you come to your final period of revision. Equally, you may not find one particular style which works most effectively for you, and instead may prefer to employ different techniques for each subject - this is, again, completely normal. Small tests set in-class by your teachers provide the perfect opportunity to trial different memorisation methods over the course of the IB, and across subjects, so make the most of these occasions to establish your preferred technique.

3.10 Passing/Failing

The IB Diploma Programme has a number of failing conditions which catch some students unawares each year, and which it is important to bear in mind throughout your IB studies. The baseline conditions to be awarded the Diploma are (1) to attain 24 points from the six academic subjects *and* the two core components which contribute to points - Theory of Knowledge and the Extended Essay - and (2) not to be found guilty of academic misconduct (including plagiarism).

Any students who attain fewer than 24 points will not be awarded the full Diploma. In addition, any student who is awarded an 'N' (not graded/submitted) for any subject or core component, or who is awarded an E in either of their EE or TOK will fail the Diploma, regardless of other scores achieved. This is also the case for any student who is given a 1 in any subject, more than two grade 2s, or who attains a 3 or below four or more times.

If a student's Higher Level subject points total fewer than 12, or their Standard Level points are 8 or below, they are not eligible for the full Diploma, unless they have taken only two SLs, in which case their SL total must be 5 or higher. If a student has completed four HLs, only the three highest HL grades are counted towards the HL total, which must be 12 or above in order to be eligible for the full Diploma.

Finally, any student – even if they achieve the full 45 academic and core points – will not be awarded the Diploma if their CAS requirements are not completed. Every year, in the IBO's statistical bulletin, there are one or two very highly achieving candidates who are not awarded the Diploma, and they will have fallen foul of one or more of these failing conditions. An IB Diploma student has a maximum of three exam sessions to satisfy all the requirements for the Diploma, but these can be split over a number of available sessions- they do not have to be consecutive!

3.11 Unpicking a syllabus

An IB subject syllabus is the fundamental framework from which all schools teach IB subjects. The sooner you get to grips with each subject's syllabus, the better chance you give yourself of understanding what can be examined. This ensures you are being taught the correct information in school.

Each school will both teach and examine subject matter in different ways, so you should view the syllabus as your fail-safe – regardless how the content has been taught at school, if you can go through each subject's syllabus, you can feel confident ahead of your exams.

IB subject syllabi tend to change every seven years, as part of the IB's attempt to stay present with current phenomena, educational developments, and the demands of a changing world, particularly in relation to the integration of technology into every aspect of life. They try to avoid the 'used bicycle' phenomenon where you buy a new bicycle, but you don't get rid of your old one, so you slowly pile up old bikes in your garage even though you don't need them (read: old content in your syllabus)! IB Maths Standard is a good example of this, with a shift away from things like matrices (Graphing Calculators

made these impractical) and more towards more functions and calculus over different teaching cycles.

Understanding a syllabus is particularly important for STEM subjects. For the Sciences in particular, a useful exercise is to go through the entire syllabus and look up 'define'. It is incredible how often definitions are asked for as 'freebies' in science exam questions, so you're doing yourself a disservice if you aren't reviewing definitions until you can quote them in your sleep.

Syllabus Advice (particularly for STEM)

Review the "assumed knowledge"/"prior learning" section of the syllabus. Schools will often skip over this content due to limited teaching hours, so it is your responsibility to ensure you're comfortable with this content

- Check how many teaching hours are allocated to each topic -Calculus is 40 hours out of 150 in total for Maths SL, for instance, giving you an indication as to the percentage of Calculus questions which you can expect in IB Maths SL exams. This should also help you allocate your studying time both during your IB journey and ahead of exams
- Before mocks and final exams, take a fresh copy of the syllabus, and run through each line item, ticking it off if you feel confident with the subject matter, or highlighting areas you feel uncomfortable with. In doing so, you can visually see your problem areas and set a revision schedule
- Download, print, and store a copy of the syllabus for each subject you're studying at the front of your folder. As you progress through your studies, you can tick off topics you've covered, gaining a sense of accomplishment and always having a steer of how much is left to do. You will also realise if you, or your class, is falling behind, particularly for HL subjects.

In short, the syllabus should be used as revision tool, and a progress tracker through your IB studies- it is naïve not to use it to your advantage! They are easily accessible online or through the IB store.

3.12 Time Management

One of the first questions we ask prospective tutors is what they think the defining attributes of successful IB students are. Without fail, as outlined previously, the first thing they mention is time management. With such a heavy workload spread across six academic subjects and three core requirements which demand ongoing consideration, it is imperative that students are prepared for all assignments and deadlines. We have compiled a free IB-focused calendar which includes suggested IA draft deadlines, IB submission deadlines and IB exam dates, to name but a few, and would recommend downloading this, or requesting a printed copy, such that you can begin mapping out the rest of your IB journey as promptly as possible!

3.13 Working with your teachers

During our many hours of working directly with students from a broad range of schools and backgrounds, one of the most frustrating comments or complaints we hear is "but my school didn't teach it well" or "my teacher didn't tell me what to do."

By embarking on an IB journey, it is vital to take ownership of your work, and your results. The programme is sufficiently well laid out that the onus is really on you as the student to set your working schedule, and to ensure you're up to speed with the syllabus, your deadlines, and more. See school as a (very useful!) resource. They are there to help, they're the boat, but you're the captain. You need to make your own judgements about which teachers you work well with, and which subjects you feel you need to do extra work for, to ensure you aren't slipping behind the global IB standard, let alone your school's standards. Be aware, however, that taking ownership of your own learning and achievements not only involves working hard on your own, but also asking for help and guidance when required. Be your own best advocate, but be sure to look after yourself and do not try to do everything yourself!

3.14 Working with your school

Choosing the right subjects for you, to match your skills, plans, and interests, is one of the most important stages of the IB journey (*see 2.6.2* on subject selection). Not every school will offer the perfect combination of subjects for you. You may have the option of following certain subjects through Pamoja, or through self-study and working alongside external tutors, but working on the premise that you will be taking all six subjects with teachers from your school, it is your job to speak to the teacher leading each class you're planning to take **before** starting your IB studies.

Your teachers are there to help you, but there will naturally be occasional personality clashes, or you may not benefit from the style of teaching of a certain teacher. Be sensible with your subject selection, pick subjects both based on your own aspirations and to match those teachers who you feel you will learn most from and benefit from both academically and more generally. In particular, where possible, ensure your Extended Essay supervisor is someone you get on very well with. If you are changing schools to begin your Diploma studies, it may be slightly more difficult to guarantee you work well with each of your teachers before commencing the IB, but get as best a gauge as you can at information evenings and pay particular attention over the first fortnight of the IB, where it may still be possible to switch classes or even subjects. Do also try to speak with siblings, friends, and other alumni of your IB school, to see if they have particular memories of specific teachers- but do remember every personal relationship is different, so that Biology teacher who never quite gelled with your sister might be your favourite when you start the IB!

The IB is difficult, so be clever about who you want helping to guide you through the process.

Remember, be accountable for your choices, your studying habits, and ultimately your results. University admissions officers won't care who your teachers were or if they taught you the wrong material!

3.15 Working with your parents (for students)

If you are lucky enough to have supportive parents, try your very best not to be a 'moody teenager', and to engage with them through your IB studies. If they are willing to help, try to pick their brains for advice on essay writing, time management, and more, making use of the skills they have probably acquired in the working world. It can be easy to forget that your parents and the other adults in your life lead an entire life before you came along, and have continued to develop their skills throughout your life, so do be sure to speak to them before you're in a late-night essay rut to find out what they can and can't help you with.

Be honest and open with your parents if you're struggling with workloads and deadlines. The longer you can foster a transparent relationship, the less you'll feel that you are dealing with everything yourself. IB deadlines can suddenly mount up, so don't make the mistake of blocking your parents, or older siblings, out early on in journey. You will want their help at some point! No matter how well you manage the Diploma, it is very likely there will be at least one point where you feel like you're juggling too many things at once. If you have been honest and open with your family they will be able to support you through the rough patch, and will be better

placed to fight your corner at school, should you need some extra help.

3.16 Supporting your IB child(ren) (for parents)

It can be difficult to know the best support to provide to your children as they move through the IB Diploma- and as their learning becomes (hopefully!) more and more self-driven, what you need to know, and when you should voice opinions or step in to help. We have worked with countless families and students through the years, and while we have learnt that every family is unique, there are key experiences which bind almost every IB student – the deadlines will come thick and fast at the beginning of IB2, exams creep up on you and revision feels insurmountable, and university application deadlines could not come at a worse time, no matter when this deadline really falls...

We suggest being aware of your own strengths and weaknesses- if you love debating political topics with your children, you might prove to be of most use to a History student at the beginning of essay writing, whereas if you are a stickler for detail, perhaps offer to proof their essays and check their references and grammar. Try not to impose your opinions on how things *ought* to be done based on your own experience and education, but it is worth discussing the help you can provide before it becomes absolutely necessary. Where you struggled with particular topics in your own education, it is important not to pass these down to your children- whilst Maths really might have been your least favourite subject, try to avoid the "well I wouldn't even know where to start, I've never understood *x*" conversations, and instead look to problem-solve together- you might even learn (or re-learn!) something, and your child will learn most from watching you unpick something in order to be able to tackle it.

IB Diploma students are testing out their independence in anticipation of moving away from home, starting their career, or beginning university, and so there will always be little bumps in the road where your ideas on their capabilities are different to theirs. Particularly for the IB, time management and organisation are so key- a realisation which many IB1 students find towards the end of the year, rather than right at the beginning, to the eternal frustration of IB teachers and often parents! We suggest keeping a gentle eye on deadlines - perhaps agree weekly times to run through Managebac or a school calendar together to check deadlines for the week were met, and discussing the week upcoming - but would avoid going over the student's head to speak directly to their teachers about extending deadlines, or for extra information on homework set. An open dialogue should serve to teach your child about time management with a safety net of accountability, with the net (again, hopefully!), shrinking throughout the IB.

Finally, the IB is hard- sometimes really, really hard. Some stress is, unfortunately, a given for all IB students, but do keep an eye out for sharp increases in stress, or sudden lack of communication, so that you can provide any extra help or support as needed.

3.17 Maintaining a positive mindset

Exam season can be exceptionally stressful. Here's our advice to make sure you're looking after yourself while doing your very best!

With deadlines, exams, IAs, and EEs, it can feel like there's so much to do it might overwhelm you. It's important to give yourself the breathing space to do well while maintaining a positive attitude and approach to revision and work, which allows you do your very best, without the risk of burning out or pushing yourself to your extremes.

We've compiled some key advice to help you support yourself during the *hecticness* of the exam period, but you should **always** try to speak with friends, family, a teacher, or a mental health advocate if you're feeling anxious or like you can't cope. You can find more information about organisations to contact at the bottom of this article.

Don't compare yourself to others, only yourself

Working on the same material, day-in day-out, with the same people, makes it easy to constantly judge your progress against your peers. It can be useful to look around and see where other people are, but with each person having such a different background and skill set, sometimes this kind of comparison may not be very helpful.

Instead of placing yourself in comparison to your friends and classmates, focus on comparing yourself to *you in the past* and seeing the progress you've made. Everyone starts out at different stages and so by judging your own progress, and not how you compare to the best in the class, you don't lose sight of how far you've come.

Train your body, as well as mind

Plato said *"the body is the tomb of the soul."* Neglecting your physical health can have a big impact on your ability to stay in a positive frame of mind. Not sleeping, getting by on a poor diet, and hardly moving all day can exacerbate feelings of anxiety. Apps like 'SleepCycle' and 'FocusKeeper' can help your sleep patterns or ensure you take regular breaks. Apps like 'Zombies, Run!' – as an alternative to 'Nike+' – can help distract you from thinking about mitosis or microeconomics while you exercise, or 'Carrot' will jokingly insult you until your fighting-fit with short workouts you can do at home between revision sessions.

But you don't need to become a triathlon competitor to stay healthy. Drink lots of water (instead of coffee or energy drinks); take regular breaks during which you get up and move; use the '20:20:20' rule to prevent eye strain (look at something 20 meters away, for 20 seconds, every 20 minutes), and you'll begin to feel the difference.

Reward yourself

Exams are important: the have an impact on what you can do in the future, and you should try your best to succeed in them. But they're not the only things you should focus on. Motivate yourself with post-exam rewards to celebrate all your hard work and help drive that final push: go the cinema after your exam with other people from your class; order a pizza to the park and relax for a few hours. After your final exam, celebrate in a big way – have a party, go on holiday. Don't forget that exams aren't the be-all and end-all, life continues after they're finished!

Make space for revision

Revising in your bedroom is a big no-no. It's easy to get distracted: that poster of your favourite band leads to putting on their album to revise to, then you remember how good the video is for *that* song, then you're watching *all* their videos, reading the comments and you've lost hours of revision time. Then, when you close your laptop and try to sleep, all you think about is the revision you haven't done. Find somewhere else to revise – the dining/living room, the study, your school/local library – and work there. That way, you don't associate your bedroom with work (or get distracted by the things in it), but think of it instead as a work-free zone where you can truly relax.

Communicate with others

Make it clear to your friends and family that you're revising and can't be interrupted, but also make clear when you're free and *can* talk, have a coffee, or eat lunch. It's another way to motivate yourself through your sessions ('Just 30 mins and then I can have lunch with my friends') and keep you distraction-free while you work, without boxing yourself away for weeks on end.

Use these opportunities to speak with other people about how you're feeling too. If you're stressed, and feel like you *just can't* do any more work, speak with friends who are going through the same situation as you. Mums and Dads always want the best for you, and probably don't know the amount of work you have to do. School friends and teachers can help you balance your time well and advise you when to take a break, all the while from a vantage point of knowing the amount of material you may still need to cover, and how much work can be reasonably covered in a day.

If you're struggling to stay positive at any time, you should speak to family, friends, or a teacher. If you feel like you don't have someone to talk to, you can contact organisations like YoungMinds, or speak with other students on platforms like MeeToo.

3.18 Resources

Textbooks

It's not ideal to rely on one textbook, or more specifically, one resource. Different IB textbooks will vary slightly with regard to examples and how they outline each topic. If you are concerned about costs, you may want to consider purchasing IB books with a group of friends and sharing them between you. Worked example books are also incredibly helpful for Maths & Science subjects.

Too often students attain consistently high marks in the classroom but are disappointed by results in their mocks and final IB exams. Using a variety of resources is your best bet – this will keep your brain stimulated and through doing this, all the 'gaps' should be filled. However, it cannot be stressed enough how critical it is to look at past papers- so we're saying it again! Try to replicate exam conditions – print off past papers, time yourself, and don't look at your notes. How you perform on these papers is by far the most accurate way of tracking your progress and predicting what your final mark will be. Once complete, learning how marks are given on IB exams is also paramount. Get access to markschemes and learn the difference between an 'A' mark and an 'M' mark. It is amazing how much the assessment criteria can vary between a Paper 1 and a Paper 2 in the same subject!

Revision courses

Perhaps the most obvious reason for suggesting revision courses is because it is incredibly useful to spend a *concentrated period of time* drilling the key facts, themes, formulas, studies, etc. into your brain to ensure that you consolidate the knowledge you've been acquiring throughout months of learning. However, and perhaps most importantly, through taking revision courses you are exposed to a *completely different style of teaching.* No two teachers have the same teaching approach! The 'aha!' moments experienced by students typically occur when they do not *know* that they have not actually fully understood a topic – or worse, have misinterpreted it. This is because the obvious problem areas are commonly recognised and dealt with, either through tuition or independent research and practice. In summary: *you may discover new problem areas* you did not know you had, plus you'll have the time and guidance to make these your strong points!

EIB Education run Revision Courses at key points throughout the year- please have a look on our website to see if you could benefit from one of our IB or university admissions courses!

4.
Before the IB

4. Before the IB Diploma

4.1 What is the MYP?

The IB's Middle Years Programme, or MYP, is a five-year programme for students aged 11-16, which requires students to complete studies across eight subject areas, as well as an interdisciplinary subject and the Personal Project. Schools can opt to offer an abbreviated form, of two, three, or four years, but it is only the final year which contains an externally assessed aspect of the course, resulting in the MYP Certificate. The eight subject areas are marked from 1-7 for each, making the highest possible total score 56, and attaining the Certificate is dependant on completing the necessary externally assessed assessments ("eAssessments", as these are all carried out on a computer), the Personal Project, and the e-Portfolio, which contains all internally assessed, summative, work. Since 2017, the Personal Project must be externally moderated, while schools can opt to register for externally assessed exams in the rest of the MYP's subjects. Although students can only attain the Certificate if they sit the exams, course results are produced for each MYP student, regardless of their participation in the eAssessments. This can result in schools opting not to enter their students for the final assessments but providing full MYP teaching throughout the 11-16 years, with students graduating with MYP course results but not an externally validated Certificate.

The MYP (Middle Years Programme) sits between the PYP (Primary Years Programme) and the IBDP or CP (IB Diploma Programme or IB Career-related Programme), providing support for students aged 11-16, as part of an International Baccalaureate education.

As of 2017, the PYP was being taught in 1,472 schools in over 100 countries. The IBDP was taught in 2,666 schools in over 130 countries, and growing at a rate of 8% year on year over the past 3 years. The MYP is taught in over 1300 schools, having grown steadily since first reaching 1000 schools in 2013. However, in 2017, only 9% of final-year MYP students were entered for the Certificate, in comparison to 50% of Diploma students sitting for exams in May 2017. So why the disparity?

One of the main issues the MYP has faced is not having any externally moderated exams. Due in part to the MYP's previous lack of external moderation, and particularly in cases where schools or parents feel exam practise is vital in years leading up to the IB Diploma's final year exams, alongside the view that externally moderated exams are crucial for university admissions , the MYP has struggled to gain the traction the IB had hoped for over the past decade. Further, while parents seem to support the MYP's teaching style and methods, and therefore want their children to be immersed in an MYP education where possible, increased demands on children, particularly in relation to their measurable attainment, mean that some schools feel MYP teaching is best supplemented by other, externally moderated, exams. This had led to the phenomenon common in may UK independent schools, where MYP teaching is continued through the 11-16 years, but the final two years are also spent focusing on passing GCSEs and/or IGCSEs, to ease the transition out of an IB education if desired.

Which IB school?

We've compiled profiles for IB schools

around the world, with information like

average IB score, fees, and IB programmes

offered on our website at

eibeducation.com/ibschools

Key Facts

Key facts about the MYP eAssessments

- Exams last two hours, completed using a laptop or similar device
- Schools do not need to offer the eAssessment just because they offer the MYP
- Not all students need to sit the eAssessments
- The Personal Project (see below) is the only mandatory component of the MYP
- Whilst the exams themselves are assessed on a computer, internet access is not required, as the tests are sent a month prior to the exam date so that schools can download them and make them accessible to their students offline
- Students can use their own laptops or devices for the assessments
- Students must complete 8 eAssessments, which include on-screen examinations in Language and Literature, Individuals and Societies, Mathematics, Science, Interdisciplinary learning, plus ePortfolios in Language Acquisition, the Personal Project and one of the following: PE, Arts or Design.
- Each eAssessment is weighted equally so that the maximum total score for the MYP certificate is 56 with a grade of 1-7 being assigned to each eAssessment (8 x 7=56).
- Students must attain at least 28 points across these 8 eAssessments, with no grades below 3, to be eligible for the MYP certificate
- A maximum of three examination sessions is allowed in which to satisfy the requirements for the award of the IB MYP Certificate.

- Average overall total as of May 2017: 35.75 (out of a maximum of 56)
- Average subject grade (May 2017): 4.5
- Pass rate (May 2017): 75.92%

4.2 MYP eAssessments

Tim provides his thoughts on eAssessments and the future of IB assessment

I love the idea of students not becoming too exam focused, too early. The UK system of having 11+ and common entrance (13+) exams, not to mention admissions testing aged 8 in some instances when looking to gain entry to many public schools in the UK, means that a school's focus can easily move away from teaching and more towards the 'old school' chalk and talk method of rote learning and memorisation. This sits completely at odds with the IB's philosophy, and in light of this, two of the MYP's central educational concepts are:

- Discouraging a rigid curriculum and allowing the school to use their resources as best they can to cover core concepts, whilst encouraging independent thought; and
- Ensuring that students who are not focused on their final grades, or exams, and rather encouraging them to develop curiosity around the subject matter for longer-term educational merit.

Whilst I fundamentally agree with the idea, it is a slightly utopian view of education, and the lack of uptake of the MYP in schools meant the IB had to make some kind of shift. The eAssessment fixes this problem.

As per the subject brief:
"External assessment is an optional feature of the programme. MYP eAssessment has been developed for students and schools that need external verification of student achievement at age 16. The new assessment model strengthens the continuum and offers students formal, recognized qualifications"

Reading between the lines, they are trying to create a shift away from focusing too heavily on exam taking, and more on the underlying learning potential of all students. In the IB's own words: *"the MYP is focused on **learning how to learn"**.*

The eAssessments are in effect, "un-studyable". The lack of a rigid curriculum, existing of past papers and in particular, the way that questions are formatted supports this. This concept is not a new phenomenon, but one which is encouraging. As time passes and more past examples become available, it may become increasingly difficult for examiners to create unique questions in this way. The shift to computer based exams also begs the question as to whether the IB Diploma exams themselves may ultimately become assessed through computers – I don't think anyone would be surprised if this were the case in the next 5 to 10 years!

As with any new system brought in, there has been a bit of backlash from students, and many schools who initially took the programme on, and offered eAssessments, have subsequently backed out in the second year. This is a bit disappointing, but the logic is understandable. No one wants to be the guinea pig, if your grades are to remain on your transcript, and with so many parents and teachers so used to tried-and-tested exams methodologies, it will take time for schools and parents to fully invest in this new system.

Personal Project
Unlike the eAssessments, the Personal Project is a mandatory component of the MYP, and is externally moderated.

The Personal Project is a wonderful initiative for independent thinking, and interdisciplinary learning. The MYP's brief for this is comprehensive, and the fundamental idea behind these projects are very well geared towards many components of the IBDP and indeed university study.

"The Personal Project formally assesses students' ATL skills for self-management, research, communication, critical and creative thinking, and collaboration"

In terms of moderation, as with MYP & IBDP exams, a selection of projects are sent off for moderation, so that all school's grades are moderated accordingly.

4.3 The MYP: going forward

The IBO typically modifies curricula every three-seven years, making small modifications to content, and trying to update it to stay up to date with recent phenomena. There is undoubtedly a shift taking place across the educational world globally at the moment, and arguably the MYP is making great strides in the right direction, changing outdated teaching methods by "encourag[ing] connections between studies in traditional subjects and the real world."

For families deciding whether the MYP is the right route for their child, we believe there is no better preparation for students looking to complete the IB Diploma in later years, and, although it will vary from school to school, and indeed from student to student, the holistic nature of an MYP education makes it invaluable for later IB Diploma study.

Over the next few months, we will be undertaking a big project to create mock eAssessments for students to get a feel for how these will work in practice, and look forward to welcoming you back to find out more about these in due course.

4.4 The MYP and UK schools

One big question facing schools, is how best to approach 'creating' a curriculum. The curricula set for the courses are quite open. You need only compare the MYP Maths curriculum with the IGCSE Maths curriculum, for example, to establish this.

This may put off some schools, who prefer a more set curriculum, but the benefit is that if you are already running a set school curriculum, you needn't make huge changes to adapt to the MYP programme, which is quite a unique opportunity. On top of this, although there are textbooks which have been developed, teachers and tutors can realistically draw from textbooks which schools may already have to achieve the same goal, not to mention a swathe of online resources now available.

4.5 IGCSE

Before beginning the IB Diploma Programme, there are a range of programme or methods of teaching which students may take, often depending on their school's choice - students rarely switch educational systems based on the exams they will take at 16, while many students do actively choose the IBDP, and so it can be difficult to know whether you are prepared enough for the IBDP. For many students, the key choice is between the MYP, as outlined previously, and IGCSEs.

IGCSE, or International General Certificate(s) of Secondary Education, refer to a curriculum of study, in English, of a range of subjects, and prepare students for further post-16 study, such as the IB or A-Levels. IGCSEs are not a programme of study in the same way as the MYP, as students are free to choose the combinations of subjects they wish to study, although many schools do enforce a number of compulsory subjects, such as English, Maths, and Science, and are graded from A*-G, with passing grades beginning from C.

However, it is possible to ensure IGCSE students follow a broad range of subjects- the International Certificate of Education is offered by Cambridge International Education, the leading board offering IGCSEs, and is awarded to students who attain seven subject passes across five subject groups (and two in Languages!).

IGCSEs are characterised as a programme of linear learning- they are generally assessed by exams at the end of the course, which are externally marked. However, subjects which require a variety of assessment methods, such as language orals or science practicals, will not be wholly assessed by examination at the end of the course. Exams can be split into Core/Foundation exams, where C-G grades only are attainable, and Extended/Higher exams, where candidates can achieve A*-E. Candidates who fail to reach the lowest grade for their exam (G or E) are awarded an 'ungraded'.

IGCSEs are common in the UK's independent school sector, with new governmental reform of GCSEs meaning that state schools can no longer offer IGCSEs in many circumstances- academies being the biggest exception, although this is dependant on exterior funding, as IGCSE results are no longer included in a school's league table statistics and schools cannot received state funding for IGCSEs. Prior to this, IGCSE exam registration had been rising across all school sectors in the UK, particularly as IGCSE results were accepted for the English Baccalaureate.

5.
After
the IB

5. After the IB

N.B. *This section focuses on the IB and UK universities, due to our extensive experience in this area.*

5.1 The IB & UCAS

Tim's reflections on UCAS and the IB, drawing on almost 15 years' experience.

My journey

I went through the UCAS application process back in 2004, and through EIB Education I have been lucky enough to support students, predominantly in the Science areas, through their UCAS applications for many years since. A lot has changed since 2004! As an EU resident, my university fees were around £1,000 per year, and at that time applicants had the luxury of *six* choices.

With university fees on the rise, more students globally applying to the UK every year, and with now only five UCAS choices, the process shouldn't be taken lightly and, as with anything, the more you know, the better placed you are to make an informed decision. We have compiled a useful matrix which allows you to compare major degree entry requirements at the UK's top 50 universities - see our website for the most up-to-date version of this.

Resources
IB UCAS Matrix
Our IB UCAS Matrix has the entry requirements for the top 50 UK universities for the most popular subjects.
eibeducation.co.uk/matrix

Selecting your IB subjects

When it comes to the IB, selecting your six subjects is tough enough – your school may enforce their own requirements to allow you to take certain subjects, whilst classroom timetabling and teaching quality all come into play. On top of this, it is down to you to investigate whether certain universities have specific subject requirements alongside a total IB score. When selecting your subjects, you must strike a balance between enjoying what you are learning whilst ensuring you aren't missing out on key course entry requirements. Think you'd like to study Medicine - make sure you're taking HL Chemistry and Biology, and are on track for at least a six in both throughout your studies.

How does UCAS view the IB?

This brings up the important discussion as to how the IB stacks up against A-levels, and how you can ensure you use the IB's strengths to your advantage when making your applications to UK universities. The table below shows a rough comparison of how the new UCAS weighting pits IB students against their A-level peers:

IB Score		UCAS Points	A-Level Grade
At HL	At SL		
7		56	A*
6		48	A
		40	B
5		32	C
	7	28	
4	6	24	D
	5	16	E
3	4	12	
2	3	0	
1	2	0	
	1	0	

Confession: I have never sat an A-level exam. But in my early tutoring career, I reviewed many exam papers, and I think the A* = 7 points at HL comparison is quite fair. The grading breaks down slightly after this, but there are a couple of points which I find confusing, and potentially ill informed:

1. A 3 at HL provides 12 UCAS points, which is the same as an A for your Extended Essay. Anyone who has worked hard for 2 years at an HL subject only to perform poorly in their exam will know that the hourly commitment alone means a 3 at HL merits far more points than an A grade for the Extended Essay.
2. The SL weightings generally seem undercooked. 28 points for a 7 at HL (in a subject such as Maths Standard, which is only marginally 'easier' than A-Level Maths) appears slightly underweighted.
3. Bearing this grading weighting system in mind, as far as UCAS is concerned, 36 points does not necessarily equal 36 points, depending on your grade breakdown at HL vs. SL. Confusing, I know!

Ultimately, **these UCAS weightings are there to serve as a barometer for universities to compare a plethora of applications** arriving on their desks from all around the world, and it is the total IB predicted score, and not the UCAS tally that you should focus on. To learn more, it is always worth playing around with the UCAS tally calculator.

Despite a couple of anomalies, I would argue that UCAS "gets" how difficult the IB is, but that universities are still playing catch up. This is improving year on year as more and more IB students apply through UCAS. The old UCAS weighting system effectively said that 45 points was the same as 5 A*s and an A at A-level. I know a few 45 pointers, but have never met anyone with 5 A*s and an A at A-level. Moreover, **the IB's consistency in approach offers a robustness that A-levels have lacked over recent years** – the introduction of the A* and the Extended Project Qualification (EPQ) all smack of a search to offer more diversity and move away from what is viewed as quite a staid educational system. While these seem like good ideas, and are viewed by many as an attempt to replicate the IB structure, the recent changes to AS

levels are very confusing, for students and schools alike.

Timing

All of the above should help contribute to making your final choices, and give you confidence as to how well regarded the IB is both at UCAS, the central application body, and indeed by universities themselves. But perhaps the most discernible benefit of being an IB student comes on 6th July, IB results day, and the day after Clearing opens. If you haven't quite hit your marks, you have a full 5 weeks to make contingency plans before A-level results come out in mid-August. You can call up your Firm and Insurance universities to find out if you are still allowed to take up your space. In all likelihood, they will ask you to wait until 15th August, but in that time you can start investigating your plan of attack for Clearing, or even consider retake options long before A-level students know how they have performed. This little known timing benefit is an ace in the hand for IB students looking to enter tertiary education in the UK. For further information on Clearing and Adjustment, *see 5.6.*

There are 4 key deadlines to be aware of.
1. Your Year 1 (IB1) mock exam dates
2. 15th October, the UCAS deadline for Oxford, Cambridge, Medicine, Dentistry, and Veterinary Sciences applications
3. 15th January, the UCAS for all other courses
4. 6th July – IB results day

Resources
Year Planner
You can download or order a copy of our Year Planner for free on our website, it has all of the key IB dates you need to know!
eibeducation.co.uk/calendar

IBDP1 Exams Are Key
Many students don't fully acknowledge the importance of their end of year exams in their first year, and do this at their peril! Most northern-hemisphere schools go back in session in late August or early September, which means there is little

opportunity to gauge any performance change between IBDP1 mocks in June, and UCAS submission in October or mid-January. As such, **your predicted grades are heavily informed by these grades, meaning your IBDP1 mocks are as important, if not more important, than your final IB grades.** The logic here is that if you are under-predicted based on poor mock grades, you will have to apply to universities with lower entrance requirements, so why score highly on your final exams if you end up at a mediocre university anyway?

The two UCAS deadlines should also be considered, even if you aren't looking to apply to Oxford or Cambridge (Oxbridge). For example, if you feel your predicted grades may slip between October and January due to your focus shifting to TOK & EE submissions, why not apply early? And conversely, if you feel there is any chance of boosting your predicted grades, wait as late as possible up until 15th January to give yourself the best chance of offers, based on improved predicted scores.

Making your 5 choices

When it comes to making your final 5 choices, I advise a "**5 point spread**". That is to say, your highest and lowers entry requirements, should have at most a five point difference between them. It is up to you to establish what your final predicted marks are, but if you're confident that your prediction is 36 from conversations with teachers, you may want to risk your first choice being a 37, and therefore your lowest insurance a 32 - with a spread of points in between. In doing so, you are both giving yourself an insurance policy, whilst also taking a calculated risk. After all, you don't want to play it too safe and end up at a university below your academic standards. Likewise, selecting five universities all with suggested scores of 36/37 won't help you either.

Assuming you receive all five offers, how best do you approach that situation? **Gaining a strong understanding of how the 'Firm' and 'Insurance' policy of UCAS applications works here is vital**, and

I would advise reading thoroughly through the UCAS advice on their website on this matter.

But where should I go?

City vs campus? Red brick or shiny new-build? Russell Group? A good sports programme? There is so much to consider when making your final five choices, and too many universities to properly debate the merits of here. I would strongly advise ordering copies of university prospectusus early, speaking with friends who attend(ed) the universities you are considering, and - if possible - having a walk around the campuses and cities. It is amazing how much one's view can change when you compare a picture in a book with breathing in the air and seeing the undergrads having lunch in their department cafeteria.

How the IB helps you stand out

Which brings us to the most important section of this advice: how the IB helps you stand out in your UCAS application. We've gone through the dates and the UCAS weightings, but the real area of focus should be your personal statement:

1. **Your Extended Essay is gold-dust.** Make sure your title closely matches your chosen degree course title. This is the closest example to independent research you will carry out, and is exactly what university admissions officers are looking for.
2. **Focus on the S in CAS.** CAS is such a wonderful phenomenon, and being active in community work and service is a great USP on your personal statement.
3. **TOK.** Not only are you undertaking six subjects, you are also learning *about* learning, which will thrill many admissions officers and demonstrates real critical thinking skills.

Now you know (nearly!) all you need to know, **I leave you with a UCAS application checklist:**

1. Start early
2. Know your predicted grades. Need to boost a certain grade? Offer to sit an extra mock exam a couple of weeks before your submission

3. Check entry requirements early and pivot in your subject selection early – if you can. Changing from SL to HL or vice versa is very difficult more than a couple of weeks into your IB studies

4. Be aware of standardised test requirements for your degree choices, and build these into your two-year calendar.

5. Keep in mind the "5 point spread" when making your final choices

6. Let the IB do the work for you when scripting your personal statement

7. Have a plan on 6th July and be sure to make the most of your time advantage

Good luck! Everyone who has been through the IB feels part of a wider family, and the amount of information now available can be overwhelming. Make a plan, and research your options early. Learn as much as you can, make informed decisions and you can't help but succeed!

5.2 Deciding what and where to study

Bella provides guidance on what to consider when balancing your university options

Deciding what to spend the next three – or four! – years focusing on can be an enormously difficult decision, but students can fail to remember they won't just be studying while at university. University

is a time to build your own life, often for the first time, and so picking a course without considering the type and location of the university can lead to not having *quite* as wonderful a time as you may hope for. So, what should you study at university, where should you go, and is it all worth it?

So, what should you study?

This can either be the simplest or most challenging aspect of the application process. I vividly remember being deeply envious of my friends and peers who knew precisely what they wanted from life, and so opted for degree courses which would steer them on this path - Medicine, for instance, or Law. As someone whose Science option was SL Biology, I even briefly considered whether being a GP was in my future, just so that I would feel my degree was setting me up for later life – *although this flirtation with the Sciences was short-lived!*

Eventually I had to sit down with myself and consider *why* I was going to university - for me, **university was an opportunity to spend time discussing things that I love with exceptional lecturers and peers**, and was not solely geared towards my later working life. This allowed me to decide to pursue my first love, English Literature, and I began to read course descriptions at a range of universities. However, **not all applicants are lucky enough to have studied their desired course before university**– whether due to being unable to study this at their pre-university level (such as Law on the IB) or to discovering the discipline too late to have selected it as a focus when picking IB subjects. So, how do you know which course to study?

It is important to understand the *reality* of your subject area, and so while reading course descriptions on university websites is a great introduction to the differences between departments, **these won't tell you which courses require library visits late into the night most days, and which will take over your Christmas holidays as you write end of semester essays or revise for exams.** For this, find recent graduates and probe them for information! Ask them what they thought they would spend their university days doing, and what they really found themselves doing, year by year. Imagine yourself spending three years working in this subject area, and ask yourself if this sounds like fun - if it does, you're on your way!

For me, I knew spending the next few years of my life reading, discussing, and writing about books sounded like heaven- I couldn't quite believe it was a legitimate university choice and wanted to apply before anyone realised this was way too much fun to be hard work. Naturally, over the three years of my undergraduate studies and then my MA year, I did find **it is impossible to love your subject every hour of every day**, but I was studying and living in an amazing city, and so found it easy to take myself away from work and enjoy the other side of university life whenever essays became too much. Which leads me to...

Where should you study?

It can be daunting looking at the university league tables and trying to ascertain which *really* is the best for what you want to study. You may even have your top, fingers-crossed, if-everything-goes-as-well-as-it-can choice, but where else should you apply? All five choices should straddle the balance between being a department with specialisms you would like to study, at universities you consider to be well-suited to you, your interests, and your ambitions, and in locations where you would like to spend the next few years. No matter how interesting your subject, it is a rare student who can ignore poorly suited surroundings for three years and truly enjoy their time at university. Knowing whether you are well-suited to somewhere you've never lived can be very tricky, but not as hard as knowing this about somewhere you've never been.

Go to open days! I realised I could never study at a campus university while interviewing at Warwick, which was wholly too late for me to be coming to this realisation. Luckily, my other choices were city-based, and so I could opt not to take up the place at Warwick, but I could have avoided this difficulty by going to visit the campus beforehand. For students

who want to feel part of a community, on the other hand, a disparate student body in a city like London may feel alienating and lonely, and campus universities may be exceptionally exciting here. **You'll only know by visiting, so try to visit as many '*possibles*' as you can before making your final decisions.**

Do take into consideration the reputation of the universities, but do not let this be your only concern. It is harder to do well in a place that makes you unhappy, and so try to balance both your academic and personal interests when deciding where to spend the next few years.

Is it worth it?

The stress of applying to university, alongside worries about entering the job market and higher tuition fees, mean that many students are considering whether it is worth them applying to university at all. I would advise that while university is not for everyone, if you can be excited by the idea of spending three years surrounded by people who love your discipline, discussing, debating, and experimenting in your subject area – and all the hard work this entails – while building an independent life alongside this, then there may just be a UK university and course perfect for you.

If you'd like to discuss your options, or to hear more about the university experiences of any of us here in the office, please do get in touch- we're always happy to provide advice where we can, and all loved our own university studies and experiences!

5.3 Personal Statement

Writing a great Personal Statement can be tough. With only 4,000 characters, there's very little space to describe some of your more interesting academic experiences, or elaborate on your love for a subject. However, it is these features of your personal statement which will help your application stand out to admissions tutors and, hopefully, keep you in the tutor's mind and push you to the top of the pile. Consider that Oxford advises that they *"want to see that you are truly committed to the subject or subjects you want to study at university... you need to show tutors how you have engaged with your subject, above and beyond whatever you have studied at school or college."*

The first thing you need to consider when beginning your Personal Statement is the structure.

Although it is rather formulaic and bland, there is a general structure that admissions staff expect to see. This will help you in writing clearly and concisely, which is key. Try and start by writing down some of your key interests, achievements, and importantly, why you want to study the subject you are applying for and what enthuses you about the subject. UCAS offer advice and have developed a useful worksheet to help you design and structure your writing.

Once you have done this, you need to consider how you can fit your experiences roughly into the following structure:

1. What do you want to study, and why?
2. What are you currently studying, and how have your studies prepared you for university?
3. How have your hobbies, achievements, volunteering, or work experience helped you develop useful skills?
4. What are your future academic and/or career aspirations?

Which? University suggest that you focus about 75% on academics and 25% on extra-curricular activities. While this structure can be played around with a little. The main thing to try and avoid is using stock phrases, or plagiarising other pieces of work. Be concise, try and be different without always using a thesaurus, and be descriptive. Consider what James Seymour, Director of Admissions at the University of Buckingham, has said; *"a well-written personal statement with a structure that has clearly been planned and refined will not only make the information within stand out, it will demonstrate to the reader that you have an aptitude for structuring written pieces of work, a crucial skill that's required for all university courses."*

Secondly, throughout your Personal Statement you should be referring to your love for the subject, and how the experiences you're referring to are helping you develop into a well-rounded and confident student. Liz Hunt, undergraduate admissions manager at the University of Sheffield, has argued that the *"best statements will show that a student is interested in the subject; that they've studied it [or considered what undergraduate study involves], that they've developed an interest in it outside school, and that they're developing their skills and abilities outside academia."*

Remember, that this is likely to be the only impression the university will have of you outside of your academic achievements, as most will not interview. You need to make sure that you're conveying that you're interested in further study and that you have the right qualities and skills to progress. Don't be afraid to sell yourself! While not embellishing your experiences you should be constantly aware of how your experiences have helped you develop into a great student.

5.4 Oxford & Cambridge

Abby reflects on her own Oxbridge application and provides guidance for prospective applicants

This time five years ago, I was preparing my application to study **Natural Sciences at Christ's College, Cambridge.** Like almost everyone else in my position, I was certainly daunted by the prospect of Oxbridge applications. Admission is highly competitive, and, unlike most other UK universities, you have to tackle interviews and admissions tests. That said, don't let any of this put you off – if you have the predicted grades you need, and are passionate about your subject, you're certainly in with a chance! So here are my tips for anyone interested in applying to Oxbridge who's keen to maximise their chances of success.

Choosing your subject and college

You'll need to devote some time to preparing your Oxbridge application, starting with your subject choice. The workloads at Oxford and Cambridge are intense, so make sure you pick something you love (or something you're very interested in if it's a new subject), otherwise those 9am lectures will be a real struggle. Read through the course websites to see if the content and structure appeals to you.

Next comes choice of college. With 34 undergraduate colleges at Oxford and 29 at Cambridge, it can feel a little overwhelming when you come to pick. Think about what's important to you in a place where you're going to be working, socialising and living: consider factors such as location, size, accommodation options, food and facilities. (I, for instance, picked Christ's predominantly based on its central location – which turned out to be a perfectly valid concern!) If you can, it's a good idea to visit a few of the colleges to get a sense of their individual atmospheres too, so check college websites for upcoming open days, although do note that most colleges will be happy to let applicants have a look outside of these dates.

Preparing your application

When it comes to preparing your UCAS application, it's worth devoting plenty of time to your personal statement. Start writing a first draft as soon as you can, and plan to re-draft this several times before submitting your application. Oxford and Cambridge are looking for a more academic focus than many other universities, so you shouldn't spend more than around a fifth of your personal statement talking about your extracurricular activities and interests. This piece of work is a great opportunity to demonstrate passion for your chosen subject, and you can do so by talking about what you're enjoying in your current studies, any further reading you've done to deepen your subject knowledge, relevant work experience and long-term career aspirations (if you have any yet – don't worry if not!). Of course, the Extended Essay is also a useful piece of work to mention: even if it's not relevant to your chosen degree subject, the process of researching, planning and writing a 4000-word essay is an impressive skill to demonstrate in itself. Ultimately, remember that if you later receive an offer for an Oxbridge interview, your personal statement may provide the basis for some of your questions, so make sure you're confident in discussing anything you mention there.

Depending on your course, you may be required to take an admissions test as part of your application. You might have to take these tests on specific dates, and many will have a deadline for registration as well, so it's important to research them in advance.

Admissions websites often provide past papers for these tests, so try to practise them too!

Interviews

Once you've sent off your UCAS form, sat your admissions tests, and submitted any additional questionnaires and pieces of work requested, you may be offered one or more interviews with a number of academics in your chosen subject, which tend to take place in early December, unless you are arranging an overseas interview, which may take place as early as mid-October. As scary as these can seem, they really are just a chance to see how you think and whether the system of learning at Oxbridge would suit you. It's a good idea to make sure you're confident with anything mentioned in your personal statement (e.g. a book you've read), as well as the subjects you're currently studying, but you'll often be given new material to have a look at beforehand, or be introduced to novel concepts. The academics want to understand your thought process, so you should try to 'think aloud' rather than focusing on reaching the correct answer. I remember being incredibly nervous before my interviews (this is normal!), but ultimately I really enjoyed the opportunity to have a discussion with academics at the top of their field, and you'll probably come away having learned a lot. This is important because the interview system is really a taster of the Oxford tutorial or Cambridge supervision format (a key part of the Oxbridge teaching approach involving regular sessions with an academic in pairs or small groups), so be sure to remember the interview is as much of an opportunity for you to see if Oxford or Cambridge is the right fit *for you*, as well as *vice versa*.

What next?

You should find out in January whether you have received an offer. If you're unsuccessful, it can of course be disappointing, but remember that it's possible to take a gap year and reapply the following year; several of my peers at Cambridge had done this and certainly gained some valuable knowledge from their first application, so felt much more confident the second time around. Equally, as prestigious as Oxford and Cambridge are, they are just two of the many excellent universities here in the UK, and you may find yourself better suited to somewhere else. Many strong applicants don't receive Oxbridge offers but still go on to be highly successful elsewhere, so don't be disheartened.

5.5 UCAS for international students

We provide advice to international students applying to UK universities regularly, and have compiled here some key questions we receive over and over again. Should there be anything not featured here which you would like guidance on, please feel free to contact us at any time (contact@eibadmissions.com)!

Picking the right subjects

One of the main things students tend to ask about is which subjects they should choose for their Diploma. Will the chosen subjects be the right to get you onto your dream university degree, and what about if you do not know what you want to do once the IB is over?

It may also be that since choosing your Diploma options you've had a change of heart or for instance, discovered a passion for a Standard Level subject you didn't know you had. This is particularly applicable to the sciences, which at university in the UK usually have a Maths requirement for entry. We find many students suddenly find themselves facing requirements they may not have considered in the first place, such as HL Maths to gain a place to study Physics at Imperial College London. However, if this is something you would find yourself faced with, all hope is not lost. We would recommend you to look into the Sixth Term Examination Paper, or STEP for short. "STEP Mathematics is a well-established mathematics examination designed to test candidates on questions that are similar in style to undergraduate mathematics," according to the Admissions Testing Service's website.

STEP consists of 3-hour paper-based examinations – STEP 1, STEP 2, and STEP 3 – and candidates are usually required to sit either one or two of these examinations. While primarily used by the universities of Cambridge and Warwick, many other other UK Universities recognise the examination as a good reflection of mathematical ability. You can find the STEP Specification easily online, but do let us know if you have any questions on this.

You should also feel free to ring the university or universities in question. If the information on the website is unclear, or you would like the opportunity to explain your HL subjects choices in more detail, pick up the phone and ask to speak to the admissions tutor for your chosen subject.

Designing your Extended Essay

The Extended Essay is not only an extremely important part of your Diploma, but is also a very good opportunity to write something of interest to you, to show university admission tutors your aptitude and passion for a subject, and that you have the right skills to make a seamless transition to undergraduate studies. The advice from our experts Tim and Wei Hao is to pick one of your Higher Level subjects to conduct your study into, setting a title and investigation that is very specific, allowing you to specialise and explore a topic in the necessary depth.

Remember to be constantly aware of the grading matrix that the IBO has set. This will allow you not only to plan and structure your essay in a detailed and focused way, but ensure you get the top marks!

Will the IB get any easier?

As with any academic studying, the IB can be as easy or as hard as you wish to make it. There is no doubt that the content is certainly difficult, but the best way to mitigate this and stay on top of your work is to organise, organise, organise! One of Tim's top tips is to work to the syllabus, setting out all the topics that you need to know for your chosen subjects. Go through each one, be brutally honest and grade yourself on your knowledge. Are you very confident, confident, not so confident, or completely baffled by the topic? This will allow you to plan your revision, focus on areas of weakness, and ensure you dedicate the necessary time to each topic. It is, also, never too

early to begin this exercise!

Why you might need work experience

For certain subjects you will need work experience. This is certainly applicable if you want to study Medicine or Veterinary Sciences at UK universities, and might also apply if you would are applying to study for an under- or postgraduate degree in Education.

In relation to Medicine there are important reasons for this, as UK medical school want you to demonstrate the following, according to the Medical Schools Council:

- That you have had people focused experience of providing care or help to other people and that you understand the realities of working in a caring profession
- That you have developed some of the attitudes and behaviours essential to being a doctor such as conscientiousness, good communication skills, and the ability to interact with a wide variety of people
- That you have a realistic understanding of medicine and in particular the physical, organisational and emotional demands of a medical career.

The Council also advises that the importance of completing work experience is to demonstrate "what you [have] learn[ed] about yourself, about other people and about how effective care is delivered and received... make sure you show... what attributes you demonstrated and what you learned."

What if you are predicted 35 points, is it worth applying for a 36 point university?

Certainly, it can still be worth applying, as the university may also look at your personal statement and the references from your teachers to make a decision about whether to make you an offer. This information should be used as a way of demonstrating your aptitude, dedication to study, and that you hold the attributes universities are looking for.

Also be aware that the guidelines for offers set out on university websites are not final. Again, it is always advisable to ring the university to try and gain further insight into their application process, what they are looking for in students, and what will help your application stand out. With all this information, the admissions tutor may be led to believe that you would be an ideal match for their department and programme.

Why might Australian and Singaporean universities require higher grades?

Unfortunately there are still a lot of countries and institutions to which the International Baccalaureate is a new and relatively unknown qualification. However, in the UK there is widespread knowledge of what the Diploma is, how it differs to the British national curriculum, as well as other national curricula around the world. This has led to the Universities and Colleges Admissions Service, commonly known as UCAS, to recently re-evaluate the grade weighting system, reducing the weighting of IB subjects to bring it further into line with newly updated A-levels.

You can find out more information through UCAS, the IB Schools and Colleges Association, the Russell Group's guide *Informed Choices*, and Unistats.

What is the cost of living in London?

The cost of living in London is high. The British Government estimates that you will need approximately £104 per week for living costs, in addition to your accommodation costs, but this will vary depending on how much you socialise. In addition, UK Visa and Immigration controls require you to have a budget of at least £1,265 per month to study in London (on top of your tuition fees), in order to obtain a Tier 4 visa up to a maximum of nine months.

While London is certainly expensive to live in, this is countered by the access you have to amazing cultural events and institutions, many of which are free, and the excellent academic and work opportunities living in London can offer!

There are lots of tools and useful websites to help you manage your budget, and break down the costs further, of which just a few are: Study London, Brightside Student Calculator, UKCISA International Student Calculator.

UK Visa and Immigration controls

As you may be aware, there have been a lot of changes to immigration law in the UK over recent years, and this is likely to change somewhat more in the coming years as the UK leaves the European Union. To ensure you're up to date with any changes that have been made recently, we advise that you always consult the British Government's website first, as well as consulting our guide to Brexit for international students, accessible on our Consulting website.

5.6 UCAS Clearing, Adjustment, & Reapplying

Clearing

Students applying to undergraduate courses in the UK apply through UCAS, the central body who act as the conduit between individuals and their prospective universities. Should an individual receive their exam results and not meet the conditions of either their Firm or their Insurance choice, or should they simply not hold any offers by the application deadline of 30th June, UCAS provide a service called Clearing. Clearing matches students without places to university courses with spaces. UCAS also offer Adjustment, a service for students who receive their results and exceed the conditions of their Firm choice by a significant margin; Adjustment allows these students the opportunity to attend a university with higher entrance requirements.

Clearing is open to students who do not hold offers on 5th July 2016, and you will be notified of your eligibility for Clearing if your status in UCAS Track reads either 'You are in Clearing' or 'Clearing has started'; applicants without either of these messages are encouraged to contact any universities who are yet to provide their final response as swiftly as possible. Applicants who choose not to move ahead with either their Firm or Insurance choice are also able to move through Clearing, although this is a highly unusual step to undertake.

Applicants can register for Clearing from the end of June, if you are holding no offers or have no offers once your results are released. The direct contact service means universities can contact students directly from 5th July, if you have registered at this time. Clearing remains open until early September, but course places, particularly in competitive subjects, or at desirable institutions, will fill quickly.

Students search through all open vacancies through the UCAS Clearing page, and note their Clearing entrance requirements- please note that these are often lower than the course's usual requirements, so be sure to double check each one. Being certain to research each suitable and interesting course, applicants then call the Clearing hotline of their top choice, where they will speak to a member of the Clearing team, who they must convince of their genuine desire and suitability to study the course they are applying for. Successful applicants then usually are passed to an academic admissions officer, or the Clearing team member may provide a verbal

offer immediately. It is vital to impress in this phone call, and any others made in the hopes of securing Clearing offers, so be sure to prepare well, and do your research!

Since 2015, applicants have been able to sign up to an optional service ('direct contact service') whereby universities can contact them directly with an offer of a place during Clearing; if eligible, students will receive an email from UCAS inviting them to register. For all other Clearing students, however, you will not be contacted directly by universities, and instead must take the initiative and call each university you are interested in to discuss possible offers.

Inputting Clearing choices works differently than the usual UCAS choices; applicants must only enter a choice in Clearing once they have received confirmation from a university that they are holding an offer of a place from the university.. To this end, applicants can hold multiple 'offers' from universities, but can only enter one final choice into the UCAS Clearing system. Entering this choice is a firm acceptance of your offer, and you will then receive a confirmation letter from UCAS, and join the university with the rest of your cohort in September/October.

Applicants who applied to multiple courses in their first round of applications, and therefore paid the full £24, do not need to pay an additional fee for Clearing. Applicants who only applied to one course and paid the accordingly lower fee of £18 will need to pay the additional £6 to enable them to apply to multiple courses.

Clearing candidates do not hold Insurance choices, as they have received their results at the time of receiving Clearing offers. Inputting a choice into Clearing constitutes a Firm acceptance of the offer from a university, and so Insurance choices are not necessary.

Candidates may accept a verbal offer over the phone, or via email, but the final acceptance of an offer must come through the Clearing system.

Following accepting an offer through Clearing, candidates will be contacted by UCAS confirming their place, and then by their new university, who will lay out their institution's enrolment process.

Adjustment

Adjustment opens on A-level results day and is open until 31st August. Your Unconditional Firm choice stays until you confirm you'd like to go ahead with another course, and so Adjustment is a risk-free way to consider other university courses with your actual results. However, most highly competitive courses will be full by this time, so this is mainly aimed at students predicted 32 who achieved 36, rather than those predicted 37 who achieved 40.

Retakes

Retakes are increasingly common and this year first time applicants through UCAS made up 511,000 of the 559,000 applicants applying by the 15th January 2018 deadline, meaning 48,000 (8%) were re-applicants for 2018 entry! Retakes are accepted by a majority of UK universities, but most will ask you to exceed the original entrance requirements, rather than simply retake to meet these.

6.
What
We've
Learnt

6. What We've Learnt

6.1 Quick Advice

Through our combined 30 years of IB learning and many more years of providing IB tuition and advice, we have been able to compile some key pieces of advice applicable to every IB student at some point throughout their journey. Here, we include some of the nuggets of wisdom from the EIB Education office team throughout the years!

Remain focussed on the ultimate goal

Where do you want to apply for university? What marks will you need to secure a place? What type of career do you wish to have one day? Write down all of your goals on a piece of paper and hang it above your desk. Whenever you're feeling discouraged or overwhelmed, look at it and remind yourself of where you want to be. Sometimes it's necessary to look at the bigger picture and put things in perspective, but there are times when you may have to focus on the smaller targets that will get you there. Whatever the circumstance, having these goals written down will help you remain focussed and on track.

Do not only rely on your teachers

This is possibly one of the greatest pieces of advice you can receive. Remember that teachers are there to teach, mentor and guide, but they are not there to write the exam for you. Teachers are only human, and some may teach in a way which doesn't quite work for you - imagine the difficulty of tailoring your subject to twenty different students! - and so it is important to be able to teach yourself to pass the exams, and to gain different perspectives on what you are learning in class. After all, your IB results are your own, and so you'll want to feel like you took ownership of your subjects and carried on learning outside of the classroom. Your teachers will of course help as much as they can, but our take-away message is not to rely on your teachers for everything, don't take everything they say as 'gospel', and do outside reading on your own. You'll be thankful that you did.

Be prepared to make a lot of sacrifices

Presumably you and your friends will be applying to a wide range of universities, either within the UK or around the globe, for a wide range of courses. Naturally, you will all have different aspirations. The personal goals that you have to reach in order to build up to your aspiration – small or large – will therefore not be the same as your classmates'. It is important that you remain focussed on your own goal and don't let anyone side-track you. As scary as it is (we know – we've been there!) the next year or two is likely to determine the rest of your life.

Tackling the core

Two of the most challenging aspects of the IB Diploma Programme are the Extended Essay (EE) and Theory of Knowledge (TOK). Most IB students begin the IB prepared to take on their six chosen academic subjects. However, it's easy to forget that on top of these six subject choices, just as important for the completion of an IB Diploma is CAS, the 4,000 word EE project, an oral presentation, and a 1,600 word essay for TOK. As these elements present new challenges to students, it can be difficult to understand how and when to tackle the requirements for each, and for TOK in particular, the newness of the material and approaches covered can encourage students to kick their core commitments into the long grass, but these aspects of the IB are just as important as your subjects, and deserve (and demand!) your attention.

Tim, Director of EIB Education, extols the benefits of the Core Elements of the IBDP, which encourage students to "learn how to solve problems, write essays and approach research across six different subjects means students are generally well prepared to approach both their Extended Essay and TOK when the time comes." Over his many years of tutoring and running EIB, Tim has found that one skill that perhaps needs a bit of extra effort and thought is picking a very specific research question for the Extended Essay. Most students will pick quite a broad title, meaning their research is then too wide-ranging and results and answers may come across muddled.

4,000 words initially looks enormous, but having the foresight to see that this can really only touch the surface of an area of research is a skill in itself. For both the EE & TOK assessing the reputability of sources is important – with the wealth of information now available online, through Google and Wikipedia, it takes a keen eye to ascertain which routes to explore and to extract nuggets of key information in what can otherwise seem an endless supply of contradictory sources.

While completing these Core Elements of the Diploma might seem stressful, they do bring many benefits. Being able to carry out independent research is a real hallmark of the IBDP, and sets students apart from those in other equivalent school-leaving systems. As Tim points out, "it is a skillset absolutely necessary for university, and a necessary transition from some rote learning to more inquisitive and research-driven learning. As all students need to do them, it is also a nice leveller between the more humanities focused students, and more scientifically minded."

So, don't think about the EE and TOK as a tiresome task, but as an opportunity to explore areas of interest in greater depth and build useful skills. However, do begin working on the requirements for

both well in advance of your school's deadline, and do not put yourself under pressure to think creatively or create exceptional work when you are working to an incredibly tight deadline. Because remember, as Tim says, *you don't know what you don't know* - and you will only learn this by hitting a wall in your TOK essay, or when researching for your EE!

Peer-checks

Don't be afraid to discuss work with your peers. This is often most helpful when you take different subjects or are learning different topics. Have a friend who does not take your subject read your essay – does it make sense? Are there typos? Can they suggest improvements that can be made? Equally, if you and your friend(s) do take the same subject, each choose a topic you feel most confident in (or least confident in!) and take it in turns to explain it to the rest. Formulating potential exam questions for your friends to answer also proves to be a useful way of both broadening and consolidating your knowledge.

Don't panic

Everyone gets something wrong at some point- don't panic! With the many subjects, each with their own deadlines to meet, all IB students will miss a deadline or forget a piece of homework at some stage. The key thing is to take control of your mistake, prioritise fixing it, and take stock of all upcoming deadlines to ensure no 'knock-on' damage. Speak with your teacher or IB Coordinator if it is a significant deadline, and complete the work at the earliest opportunity.

Enjoy it!

As a team we all thoroughly enjoyed our IB studies, and have used the skills fostered by the IB to follow a range of academic and non-academic interests and projects; we believe the Diploma Programme is the best post-secondary educational programme available today, and encourage all those who feel they might be interested to research it and, if you ultimately decide it is for you, to enjoy every moment! We here at EIB Education remain on hand to answer all and any queries you may have, so don't hesitate to contact us with any questions you have.

6.2 Managing Stress

While the IB opens many doors for students, and all your hard work will absolutely pay off, **it can be difficult to see the wood for the trees** when in the middle of revision stress. So, how can you look after yourself, and know *which* sacrifices to make, and *when?*

It can be easy to get caught up in the ever-popular IB exam stress cycle, where you have too much work to do, and tell all your friends, who also have too much work, how much work you have, and you end up then spending all your time thinking about how much you have to do, without ever being able to sit town and tackle it, bit by bit. So, the first thing to do is...

1) Be realistic

Look at where you are in each subject, how long until each exam, and what you still need to cover in order to be where you want to be. **Make lists of every topic or key area** in each subject, and rate your confidence in answering exam-style questions in each. Once you start moving through these, be sure to update them, to see how far you've come!

2) Teamwork

Spend time with your classmates, and help to teach one another. Not only might you understand

something you had struggled with previously, but teaching others really helps to cement your knowledge in your stronger subjects, and encourages you to explain in more detail than you may to yourself. For areas you all struggle with, **break each topic into manageable chunks** and allocate each part to a person - revising, teaching, and learning in groups will help you all work through your areas of difficulty.

3) Ask for help

Your parents, teachers, older siblings, and family friends may not have done the IB themselves, but they have almost certainly been through a stressful set of exams, whether while at school, for their university finals, or in their professional lives. **Make sure you ask for help when you need it**, not only in terms of the course material, but also if you feel like you are not coping with the pressures of the IB - it can be helpful to get some perspective from someone who remembers the stress but got through it, and who now remembers it fondly. And remember, it may not feel like it now, but even the IB will pass!

3) Look after yourself

Remember to **set times where you are *not* revising**– whether this a daily jog round the park, or meeting friends for lunch and a catch-up once a week, it is *so* important to have some time away from your notes. Sleep well, eat well, exercise, and make some time for socialising, and you will find you have much more stamina for revision. It is always better to do three really positive, focused hours of revision than seven hours of half-Chemistry, half-Netflix, after all!

However, there is one thing which works better than anything for battling your nerves as you sit down for each exam...

5) Work hard

The final few weeks of your IB revision before exams will be difficult– we remember it well, and know how hard it can be to stay motivated. However, think how much better you will feel walking into each exam if you are as well prepared and confident as you can be. Take the hit for this period, and remember, you've got a long *long* summer to recuperate! And finally, be positive!

6.3 Busting IB Myths

The International Baccalaureate has been operating since 1968 and consists of four programmes which cover primary and secondary education. The most famous programme, the IB Diploma (commonly just referred to as the IB), takes place during the last two years of school. With the IB diploma increasing in popularity in recent years, several myths have risen and undermined the programme's reputation. However, any IB student knows how untrue these myths are.

'Sleep, friends, IB - choose 2'
Yes, the IB will take over a lot of your time, but by no means it is a 24/7 commitment. You don't need to give up on having friends or sleeping for the next two years - you only need to manage your time well and organise yourself. The IB is very demanding, but throughout the course there will be plenty of time for studying, going out with friends and resting. You might have less free time during exam periods, but that's the same for any other equivalent course such as A-Levels.

'IB students don't have time for their hobbies'
As mentioned above, you will have enough free time to have a personal life. Additionally, the IB encourages you to spend time on your hobbies through CAS, which aims for students to take part in creative projects, sports and various activities. With the freedom to choose their own CAS projects, students can pursue their interests and make them count for their diploma progress too - how great is that?

'The IB is for smart students only'
As the IB says, the IB diploma can be taught to anyone ages 16-19, as long as the school is licenced to teach it. That is virtually the only requirement for teaching the IB. It is designed for students of all abilities and backgrounds, and is definitely not made for students with a superior academic ability. When it comes to the IB, working hard and making an effort is more important than being a gifted student, so don't think that you need to be a genius to successfully complete the diploma.

'The IB is only for 'elite' students'
Other than age boundaries, IB has no limits on who can take part in its programmes. IB is open to accept any student who is willing to make enough efforts, and has no requirements on a student's previous education, ethnicity, or any other factors that may limit his or her ability to take part. IB provides every student equal opportunities and its diversity invites students of all backgrounds to join.

'The IB is for international people only'
Sure, the IB is typically taught in international schools, where hundreds of third-culture kids study. But the IB is taught in local schools too so everyone can have access to the programme. The IB is not exclusively for international schools, even if people believe so. Plus, loads of students at international schools have been born and raised in that country, so no, you do not need to have travelled the world or have lived in a million countries to be able to access the IB.

'The IB is broad but shallow'
Several people think that having to do six different subjects make the IB broad, thus failing to cover subjects in depth. This is not true; subject syllabi are extensive and explore each topic in depth. Furthermore, almost all subjects can be taken at either Standard Level or Higher Level, with Higher Level courses being even more thorough and slightly more difficult. The IB is not a choice of breadth over depth, but a combination of both.

'Universities don't know what the IB is'
The IB is a renowned and respected programme by universities. Most IB graduates go on to higher education, so universities are more than used to receiving applications with IB scores. If you look online, you will see universities accept the IB and have set out specific requirements - in terms of IB grades - for students to know what they need to

achieve in the IB to apply to their desired university. IB students are not at a disadvantage when applying to university.

The IB is just a university prep program

It's true that students completing the IBDP programme are well prepared for university, as IB teaches them skills such as time management, critical thinking, and collaboration, which are essential skills needed in university work. However, IB also aims to provide students useful skills for any stages in life, including flexible thinking skills, responsibility, and becoming open-minded. Also, the IB is not limited to just the Diploma Programme and has many others aimed at students of a diverse range of age, including those who are still far from entering university, such as the Primary Years Programme.

IB is just a university-prep program

It's true that students completing the IBDP programme are well prepared for university, as IB teaches them skills such as time management, critical thinking, and collaboration, which are essential skills needed in university work. However, IB also aims to provide students useful skills for any stages in life, including flexible thinking skills, responsibility, and becoming open-minded. Also, IB is not limited to just the Diploma programme and has many others aimed at students of a diverse range of age, including those who are still far from entering university.

Resources
eibeducation.com/resources

You can find all our IB Resources on our website, from Year Planners to IA guides!

6.4 Exam Checklist

Here's our checklist of the small stuff, that often get forgotten, to remember before you begin. You can download this checklist on the EIB website at eibeducation.com/checklist.

Before the exam:

These are the things you shouldn't forget to bring along with you before the exam starts. We recommend you print this list off an check off each

list before you leave in the morning for each exam!

- [ ] A spare calculator, or at the very least, spare batteries.
- [ ] A bottle of water, label removed.
- [ ] A watch - if you're far away from the exam hall clock, you might be grateful you brought your own time-keeping means - but remember no smart watches are allowed during the exam.
- [ ] Your student ID - it's no good turning up if no one believes you're you.
- [ ] Stationery - always take enough pens and pencils with you.
- [ ] Your syllabus has a set of 'key words' which explain what the question is asking you. Read and re-read these. For example "write down" means there are no marks given for working - you either know the answer or you don't, so it will most likely not impact on the next part of the question.
- [ ] Check the examination venue and time - in case the worst happens and Google Maps fails so you won't be late.
- [ ] At the start of every exam, the Invigilator will read aloud conditions and information about the exam. Listen to these instructions very carefully, and make sure you follow them!

During the exam

And once you're in your exam, breathe deeply, and:

- [ ] Write clearly, and remember that examiners need to read many scripts, so they are always thankful for good handwriting!
- [ ] Read and re-read the question; don't panic, make sure you take the time to read the question slowly, underlining key words and making sure you don't misinterpret what the examiner's asking of you.
- [ ] Make a rough time management plan by calculating how many minutes are allocated to each mark. A two hour exam, for instance, worth 60 marks allows 2 minutes per mark, and so use this estimate to prevent you spending too much time stuck on a low-mark question.

☐ Use what you're given - a formulae booklet is a gift! Learn what each variable stands for each and every formulae before stepping into your exam. It is amazing how many marks can be awarded for simply knowing what each variable means!

☐ Take advantage: knowing definitions, key terms, or key dates and facts can provide 'free' marks before you have to start creating longer-form answers. Don't over-complicate the requirements here, and make sure you utilise each opportunity to score these marks.

☐ Stay calm: There will be a moment at some point in your IB exams where you feel overwhelmed, or you are faced with the question you really didn't want to come up. Don't worry, everyone else is feeling the same about something- just take a moment to ground yourself and don't let this affect your rhythm. It's always better to skip and question and come back than to spend half the exam staring at the exam paper!

6.5 Life After the IB

Getting ready for university

The summer after completing your IBDP is a time to relax, have fun and completely forget about all the worries you once had as a Diploma student! Now that you've received your results and you've met the grades to get into the university of your choice, you have years of fun and excitement (but don't forget the hard work!) ahead of you. We asked a couple of our tutors, Anna and Daniil, both IB grads themselves, how best to prepare and relax, as well as their ultimate recommendations for getting the most out of freshers week.

It's not always clear how best to prepare for the first year of your Bachelor's degree. Different universities give different advice, or you may just be told to sit back, relax and recharge. Daniil, who achieved 44 in his Diploma and is currently studying Microengineering at EPFL, explained from his experience that "a lot of courses will start with some things you learnt in school, but at a much more sophisticated level. To prepare EPFL suggests a brochure with math theory and exercises to practice."

Anna, who scored a perfect 45 and now studies Medicine at the University of Bristol, offered more practical advice. She explained that, "no one can and should be fully prepared... Everyone is in the same boat when they arrive, and learning about the new city you're living in, and how to cope independently, is far less daunting when you can muddle through it together with some new friends." However, Anna did add that looking at the clubs and societies you might want to join, buying a cookbook and practising some dishes is a good start!

Academically, both Anna and Daniil explained that you should be well prepared and have an advantage over your peers for university study having complete the IB Diploma. Both told me that they didn't find the first year of their undergrad much more stressful than DP2, with Anna noting that the IB had prepared her well in terms of managing her time, prioritising tasks, and meeting deadlines. Daniil added that the great thing about his course is that it has allowed him to specialise in areas of interest and go far beyond the IB syllabi in Maths and Physics to explore new areas. University study has also helped Anna in developing her academic skills, as "is a lot more independent than any kind of school work. If you want to do well, it is expected that you take the initiative to go to the library/do some reading on your own."

But don't forget that university isn't just about work, you should have fun and enjoy yourself also, taking advantage of your newly gained independence!

Anna's advice for Freshers Week was to have a *"relaxed attitude! It seems like a massive step for some people to leave home and go to university, but if you just take each day as it comes and be willing to be a bit more confident in talking to new people, it will all go so much smoother."*

6.6 IB Retakes

As IB students, you may find yourself in a position where you need to retake to attain the Diploma, to increase your university options, or possibly, you just want to prove that you can gain those extra few marks. We understand that this can be a challenging and confusing time, and there certainly isn't enough information out there for students! At EIB Education we've been working for several years as the lead provider of retake support, from free resources to intensive tuition and our exceptional Retake Revision Course, and we are here to answer all your IB Retakes questions.

How many subjects should I retake?

You can retake any number of your academic subjects, as well as the core components, or any combination of these, if your subject(s) are offered by your IB World School and they are happy for you to sit each subject or component through them. Candidates can sit a subject up to three times, in three different exam sessions, which do not have to take place consecutively. If you took your exams in May originally, this gives you, for instance, November of the same year, and May of the following year to retake the exams, although not all subjects are available in both May and November sessions. Alternatively, you may wish to wait a full year before retaking any IB exam, and then opt to retake again the same November or following May. Please note that opting to sit exams for a subject at the end of the first year of the IB uses one of your three sessions, and so candidates who chose to do

this limit themselves to one possible retake session in addition to their main session.

You can also revise or complete a new Extended Essay. A new Extended Essay can be registered in the same or in a different Diploma subject. However, if you are submitting a new or revised Extended Essay in the session six months after your EE was submitted (November, for May graduates), it must be registered in the same Diploma subject. You can also retake Theory of Knowledge, but must be aware you cannot carry over marks from the TOK essay, as the prompts change year-to-year and it is an examined component.

Should I retake in November or May?

This depends on what your plans are for university and how quickly you think you can reach the level you want. For example, if you are going to university in Australia, South Africa or most countries in the Southern hemisphere, it may be best to do your retakes in November as the university academic year starts in February. This way you will not have to take a year and a half out before university, but rather just 6 months or so, however this does not provide you with an enormous amount of time to revise for your retake(s) while also re-applying to university

If the academic year for your universities of choice begins in September, then it all depends on considering your current academic level, aims for your retake subject(s), and commitment to working hard over the coming months to decide if you feel that you will be able to make enough progress before November to achieve the required grade(s). If you are not confident that the time between May and November will be enough, you should consider retaking in May of the following year. Although, please remember for UK applications that the UCAS application deadline is 15th January, and the November session results are released on 6th January. Therefore students looking to apply, or reapply, to UK unis will be able to apply to university with their concrete retake results, rather than their predicted grades- which further boosts your chances if these as well as you are hoping! (Although, you will need to weigh this against preparing your application diligently, and balancing this with making the most of your time out of formal education.)

When do I register for retakes?

For November exams, candidates must be registered by 29th July if they want to pay the lower registration fees. All candidates who register after 29th July will have to pay a higher registration fee, including a late subject fee for each subject or core element registered. The IB will not accept any candidate registrations after the final deadline of 15th October, regardless of when students first took their IB exams.

The deadlines for May exams differ from the November retake deadlines. If you are retaking in May, you need to register by 29th January to attract lower registration fees. The equivalent IB final deadlines for May retake sessions is 15th April.

For students looking to retake an exam **six months** after their last attempt (in November of the same year for May exam students, for instance), the final registration deadline is 29th July for November exams and 29th January for May exams- the later October/April deadline is often not applicable to six-month retake students, as although Coordinators are permitted to register students beyond this point, many are often not happy to do so

However, you should consider your school's final internal deadline for registration will vary, and may be much earlier; remember, also, that schools, and therefore IB Coordinators, are often not accessible throughout the summer, and therefore aiming to finalise your plans with the school before the summer holidays begin is strongly recommended. As always, then, it is best not to leave it to the last minute!

How do I register for retakes?

Candidates must be registered through an IB World School – this is vital! The school you have previously sat your exams with is the most obvious choice, but if you have moved or found yourself otherwise unable

to retake through your school, it is your responsibility to find a school who will let you retake through them. EIB can provide all the tuition for your retake, but we cannot submit your exams, register you as a candidate, or supervise your IA or other non-examined work. You should make speaking with your school's IB Coordinator a matter of top priority if you decide to retake- schools do not have an obligation to offer you the opportunity to retake through them, and so it can prove difficult to find a school willing to provide you with this chance, particularly if your current school are not happy or able to do so.

Do I retake just my exams, or do I have options to retake my IAs too?

You do not have to retake all the assessed aspects of your retake subject(s); you may just sit the exams and not change your Internal Assessments. Alternatively, your school may offer you the option of revising or redoing your IAs. In this case, your teacher will be responsible for marking the new IA(s), and must be able to confirm that it is all your own work and that it is significantly different to any previously submitted work. In order to be able to guarantee this to the IBO, students re-submitting an IA or any other non-examination-based work must attend classes at the school they will sit the retake through, making some schools wary of taking on new students who wish to re-submit their IAs in addition to sitting the final exam papers. However, you do **not** have to attend classes in order to sit the exams for one or more IB subjects, making schools sometimes happier to take on students not planning to re-do their IAs or other internally assessed work.

Where can I take my retake exams?

You can find a list of all IB World Schools and the exam session(s) in which they participate on the IB website. Please note that not all schools offer retake sessions, and that schools are not obliged to take on retake candidates. You should consult with your current Diploma Programme Coordinator, as well as calling all other local IB schools should your current school be unable or unwilling to support you with your IB retakes, and we recommend doing this as soon as possible, in order to give you the best possible chance of making the necessary arrangements in good time before the registration deadline.

Can I get my retake exams re-marked?

Your examiners will not know that you are a retake candidate, and so the re-marking process is the same for you as for any other student taking their exams that session. Do be aware that the deadline for re-marking exam papers is very soon after the release of results though! Also remember that your IB Coordinator must request the re-mark for you, and as you will have left your school, they may ask for you to pay the fee up-front.

6.7 Tutor Interviews

In our Tutor Interview series we put the spotlight on members of our outstanding tutoring team. From IB-graduates to teachers and Examiners, we share their stories and their advice about the International Baccalaureate to help you make your own IB a success.

 Zhui Ning
IBDP score: 43
University: Liberal Arts, King's College London
Teaches: Chinese, English, History

Why did you choose to do the IB?

In Singapore, where I pursued my secondary education, the two options available were GCE A Levels and IB. I knew that the inflexibility and 'drilling' methods of A Levels were unsuited to me, and I liked the IB's emphasis on the humanities and coursework, so I chose to do that.

What did you enjoy about the IB?

I loved the high standard of humanities study, as well as the generally high academic standard that the IB demands of its students – things like the Extended Essay prepared me very well for the challenges of university. The balance of assessment, between coursework and exams, was also a huge load off my shoulders and I liked

the variation and emphasis on practicality (such as science experiments and presentations for language subjects) rather than just answering questions on an exam paper. The active integration of holistic education, with CAS activities and group project demands, was also something that challenged me to step out of my comfort zone and helped me grow as a student and person.

What was the most challenging part of the IB?

Coping with all the deadlines, especially in the second year and with the subjects that I'm weaker in. There was a point where I had to submit my Maths IA draft but I was attending the Yale MUN in the USA, and we were all going mad trying to finish the draft and still prepare for our debates. I remember writing about cryptography past midnight in a room with friends, listening to rock music to stay awake. It was exhausting, but ultimately so rewarding and I wouldn't have traded it for the world!

What did you do for your CAS/EE?

For my CAS, I did a variety of activities. I volunteered with a local animal shelter and carried out some recycling activities with a local urban development company. I also carried on with activities I had before the IB, such as playing the organ and archery. We also set up a netball club in school. My school organised an overseas trip for the cohort, taking us to different countries for service activities. I went to a rural village in Malaysia, where we climbed mountains and helped the villagers paint kindergarten walls, and carried out cultural exchange activities by teaching them English while they shared with us some traditional dances and phrases.

For the EE,, I wrote a comparative essay in English A, analysing gender dynamics in Arthur Miller's The Crucible and Nathaniel Hawthorne's The Scarlet Letter. I enjoyed the process and it taught me a lot about literary theory and critical literature. However, in hindsight, I feel like I could have chosen more exciting texts, but I'm still proud of the work I did, and it helped prepare me for the standards to which I am now held in university.

What is your favourite aspect(s)/specialism?
I love the sheer range of subjects and topics that my degree offers. I'm very much a humanities specialist, and am a poor student of science, so this degree – which allows me to select almost anything in the Faculty of Arts and Humanities – is perfect for me. I love that I can simultaneously explore gender and identity in Arthurian texts and take classes in Chinese philosophy alongside also commenting on socialism in 20th century Indian literature. As a relatively new degree with a small cohort, the department is also more flexible than most and responds swiftly to student concerns and suggestions for improvement.

How did the IB prepare you for this?
I found that the academic rigour of the IBDP prepared me excellently for university, especially in researching and writing high-quality essays. I already knew how to format citations due to the IAs, and a 4000-word essay didn't faze me, unlike some of my peers who had to learn how to do all this for the first time. The Diploma also taught me to manage my time a lot better, to cope with having a hundred ongoing projects and still be able to give one hundred percent to everything.

What are your favourite aspects of the IB to teach, and why?
I love teaching English Literature. It was my favourite subject and I love finding out what texts other students study (from the broad range offered by IBO's reading list) and what they think of those texts and themes. Helping students prepare for each area of assessment is also its own challenge, and one that I relish. Sometimes, it can be a bit difficult if I am unfamiliar with the student's text, but it's also a great excuse for me to read more and research

texts that I might otherwise never think about!

What has been your greatest tutoring success?
One of my students was struggling a lot with English in her first year of the IBDP, and asked for guidance. She had little belief in her own skills in the subject. We worked together on and off for the whole year, honing her analytic and essay presentation skills, and I slowly proved to her that it was all a matter of practice and confidence, and that she had the groundwork to be a fantastic literature student. She successfully achieved a 7 in HL English Literature with my assistance, and has gone on to help others with their own IB challenges, even considering setting up a website offering notes and advice. It was an honour to have played some small part in her academic success and in inspiring her to support other IB students.

What tips do you have for current IB students?
Support your classmates and get them to support you too. You are all walking the same IB journey together and you will learn from each other as much or even more than you learn from your textbooks and teachers. Figure out university applications together. Pool your notes and resources. Share with each other if you find a useful website or database. Take up baking as a relaxation method and distribute cookies and cupcakes – look after each other!

Learn to prioritise and ask for help when needed. Do the work that is most important and that will directly affect your grade and/or understanding of a subject. Don't be afraid to ask your teacher if you desperately need an extension or a repeat explanation of a concept. If you miss a deadline, apologise and ask if a teacher can help you look over the work anyway. Learn to recognise when you are in over your head and need a second or third perspective; time management is key. Don't leave huge projects like the IA, EE, or personal statements to the last minute. Always read over your assignments and edit them. Make sure you know what IBO wants – it's outlined in the subject syllabi and you can ask your teachers for clarification.

What are your best revision tips?

Pace yourself. There are a lot of subjects and a lot to do. IB exam schedules are released extremely early and tend to follow a similar pattern, so students know that they should prepare subjects like English and Economics first, and can leave History for a slightly later date.

Organise notes thematically, rather than by topic or by date. Group related areas together to make it easier to spot patterns and formulate arguments. Always refer to and attempt past year questions.

Search the internet for useful material. The IB is a global educational framework and there are countless resources (many of them free!) for those who look for them. This can save you a lot of time in making your own notes or struggling with a concept by yourself, or if you require a timeline of events or a specific chemical table or a trick to memorising facts and formulas.

What would do you differently next time?

I think I might take HL Music instead of HL Economics. I found Economics to be duller than expected, and I wish I had the chance to explore music in an academic setting. I would also pick a more straightforward Math IA topic, rather than the fiendishly difficult cryptographic research project I was struggling with.

 Olivia
IBDP score: 45
University: English Language & Literature (2016), University of Oxford
Teaches: English, Philosophy, TOK, Oxford & Cambridge Applications

Why *did* you choose to do the IB?

I chose the IB because of its international quality. Although I did my IB in England, I had been at an international school in Spain before, and I wanted to continue in an international environment – this meant peers from all over the world and a curriculum that considered and incorporated cultural awareness into academics.

What did you enjoy about the IB?

I enjoyed being able to specialise my interests with HL vs SL classes, while still maintaining a breadth of subjects. I also enjoyed the teaching style, which encourages independent thinking and discussion, instead of regurgitation of memorised material.

What was the most *challenging* part of the IB?

Although I was glad for the breadth, the most challenging part of the IB for me was having to take Maths and a Science subject. I'm not naturally good at or particularly interested in these disciplines, but I think it was good for me long term to not give up Maths at 16, as many students do in the A-level system. It was also a challenge, and so more rewarding to score highly in these subjects.

What did you do for your TOK/EE?

Some students struggle with TOK, but I really enjoyed it. It is essentially a Philosophy class, which was one of my favourite subjects. I believe it is a great chance to reflect on why and how we learn what we do, instead of barrelling forth and learning because we are told to. I also found my EE to be quite a fun, empowering project. A bit like a precursor to a dissertation at University, it is exciting to be able to pick whatever you like to write about and to know about that topic in depth. Not to mention how the EE was *very* helpful for University applications and interviews. I studied English Literature, and so knowing a lot about Nabokov's *Lolita* was impressive and helped me seem knowledgeable and passionate about my subject.

What are you currently studying?

I have recently graduated from the University of Oxford – I studied English Language and Literature.

What was your favourite aspect of the course?

The English course at Oxford is incredible because it takes you through almost all aspects of English literature by time periods – starting from medieval poetry and running all the way up to Modernism. This was amazing, not only to learn about so many kinds of literature and time periods, but to understand how they all fit together and influence each other.

How did the IB prepare you for this?

The English Literature HL course is quite thorough, with many texts studied. And, as I mentioned, the EE was a truly excellent opportunity to go in depth with a literature topic and helped me impress my Oxford tutors in the interview.

Why do you enjoy tutoring?

I enjoy tutoring English simply because I love literature. I am passionate about the texts I am teaching and this makes talking about them engaging and fun for me. It is also, of course, rewarding when I can see a stark improvement in my students' work or writing.

What makes a successful tutor?

Though it may vary, I believe what makes me a successful tutor is the fact that I love my discipline. I know this really does translate in the classroom – often my students poke fun at my enthusiasm for a certain poem or book, but then end up, after they've learnt about the beauty or craft therein, sharing my feelings towards the works. I'm proud of the fact that I've taught many students who are 'maths oriented' or who 'don't like to read', and they have wound up being interested and engaged by their texts. On top of passion, hard work and commitment are important too. I think because I am so close in age to my students, I can really sympathise with their stress or worry that their exams or coursework won't turn out the way they want. I always go the extra mile – send extra notes, or fit in extra hours, because I know my students are relying on me.

What has been your greatest tutoring success?

I've had many students move from achieving 5s to 6s or 7s, and while this is always a success, my most difficult case to date was with a student achieving 2s and 3s who, with a lot of work, moved up to a 5! There were many factors here: a language barrier, a major lack of interest on the part of the student, and a lot of missing skills. I was worried at times that this student would fail English, but with dedication and time the student achieved success.

How did you organise your revision?

I had a high offer from Oxford so I had to ensure I met my grades – I moved methodically through every syllabus point, almost 'relearning' what I had already learnt. Often, I knew the material, but anything that was hazy I re-learnt, using textbooks, notes and working closely with friends.

What are you best revision tips?

Two big tips:

1. I cannot stress enough the importance of doing past papers. You might know all the syllabus, but if you haven't had enough exposure to, for example, the specific terminology of questions in a science paper, then you may answer incorrectly. It is even more important for essay-based subjects – I see students slip up all the time by not practicing writing essays under timed conditions. When I was revising for my English exam, I started off by scoring 4s on timed written essays, so I wrote 2 essays a day for 2 weeks, learning from my feedback, and ended with solid and consistent 7s. There is a technique to exam style writing and it takes time to master. You could have

the best knowledge of The Great Gatsby, but if you don't know how to organise and articulate your ideas quickly and effectively, you won't score very well.

2. I couldn't emphasise more how helpful the mark schemes can be. The IB hand you exactly what they want on a silver platter! But so many students don't look at how they are being graded. What are the command terms? What exactly are they asking you to do? Nail these and you will score better.

What would do you differently next time?

I scored 45, so I don't think I'd do anything differently. I worked hard, but I gave myself enough space to have plenty of time to get through the material (this meant, for example, tackling my hardest subject, Maths, on occasional quiet weekends as early as February). If you can front load some of the work, the pressure will be massively lifted nearer to your exams.

 Michael
IBDP score: 41
University: Environmental Technology (2016), Imperial College London
Teaches: Business Management, Maths, Physics

Why did you choose to do the IB?

I chose to do the IB because it was, and still is, the most comprehensive and rigorous pre-university course available for high school

students. I was also attracted to the IB because of its credibility and recognition among the universities globally.

What did you enjoy about the IB?

I enjoyed the breadth and depth of the IB, as I was able to study a wide range of subjects, from Physics to Psychology and Business Management, and even French (as a complete beginner!)

What was the most challenging part of the IB?

Similarly, the breadth and depth of the IB proved to be a challenge at times, especially with fulfilling the CAS requirements over the two years. However, I did appreciate the challenging aspects of the IB, as it prepared me for the even more challenging life of a university undergraduate and graduate student abroad.

What did you do for your CAS/TOK/EE?

For the CAS component, I acted as President of my school's Green Team (which involved organising fundraising bake sales, mangrove reforestation trips, and environmental awareness campaigns), played in the school's volleyball team, and volunteered for Gawad Kalinga in building and painting homes for the urban poor.

For the TOK component, I presented on the knowledge issue of: to what extent can art be influenced by religious beliefs? I focused on a local art exhibit in which the artist showcased Catholic figures with various pop culture and adulterated ornaments. It was quite a controversial event locally, but I was awarded the highest score. I also wrote my TOK essay on the topic prompt of: "knowledge is generated through the interaction of critical and creative thinking. Evaluate this statement in two areas of knowledge". I examined the relevance of this topic prompt in natural sciences and the arts, and was achieved top marks.

For the EE component, I wrote my essay within the Psychology topic of: "to what extent is memory decline a natural product of ageing?" This was the first piece of writing over 1,000 words that I had written and served as a good introduction to academic writing.

Why do you enjoy tutoring?

I enjoy the re-learning process of reviewing and presenting the syllabi of IB Maths and Physics. Furthermore, I believe I have a unique opportunity to encourage students to be curious, active learners on their journey through and beyond the IB.

What makes a successful tutor?

I believe a successful tutor must be, first and foremost, aware and prepared for the demands of tutoring, with regards to knowledge of the whole syllabus and exams. Additionally, a successful tutor should be empathetic towards the student, able to identify any learning gaps while encouraging and supporting the student throughout the process.

What are your favourite aspects of the IB to teach, and why?

My favourite aspects of the IB to teach are the tips and tricks for dealing with exam questions, as there really is an art to it. Simply put, if a student practices answering exam questions whilst being aided by a successful tutor, they will feel more confident in their own revision and capabilities in learning.

What has been your greatest tutoring success?

Well, I hope I have been successful in not only helping my students to gain higher marks in their respective exams, but also foster an appreciation for the subject matter and application in real life.

What tips do you have for current IB students?

I would advise any students who are struggling with their own revision to seek out help through tutoring. Frankly, asking for help is one practice that I have been reluctant to do over the years, but in retrospect, I have always been grateful for doing so. Furthermore, as the saying goes, practice makes perfect!

How did you help students organise their revision?

I organised my revision by considering my student's self-identified and quiz-assessed learning gaps, the syllabus assessment statements and the time frame with which I have for the student. Ideally, I like to cover one syllabus topic per 2-3 hour tutorial session, with 30 minutes at the end for past exam questions. I use a lot of visual aids (via Google slides) and real-life examples when conducting my online tutorials (via Skype).

What are you best revision tips?

Firstly, going through the assessment statements for each sub-topic within the respective subject syllabus will give you a strong knowledge foundation. Being comfortable teaching the syllabus topics to your fellow students would also help you to absorb the knowledge quicker and deeper. Lastly, practicing with the exam questions is great for fostering confidence in preparation for the final exams.

What would do you differently next time?

Honestly, I would have liked to be less stressed out about the final exams. Leading up to them, my sleeping schedule was highly irregular and I pretty much isolated myself in my room to study. Fortunately, as I've gone through university as both an undergraduate and graduate student, I have realised that one needs balance and mindfulness in life to be truly happy and successful. Hence, I would like to recommend to any students to take time out of your busy final exam revision to go out of the library or your room, breathe in the fresh air, and just to appreciate how much you've accomplished so far in the IB and to look forward to what is to come after.

Joshua
IBDP score: 45
University: PPE (2014), Oxford
Teaches: Maths, Physics, Oxbridge Applications

Why did you choose to do the IB?
I guess I was a generalist – I wanted to do a bit of everything! I really liked the breadth of the IB and the fact that you could do a lot more than you could with A-levels.

What did you enjoy about the IB?
I enjoyed doing lots of different subjects alongside each other. It was great to have a mix and not be doing just all sciences or humanities. I also really enjoyed the CAS side of things and the non-academic element of the IB.

What was the most challenging part of the IB?
Doing Higher Level Russian as a non-native speaker having just studied the language for one year previously!

What did you do for your CAS/TOK/EE?
I did my Extended Essay in Politics, on the Democratic Peace Problem – the puzzle that democracies don't seem to go to war with each other, but are aggressive in the way that they deal with non-democracies. I really enjoyed this opportunity to go off and research a topic that I was interested in by myself. Plus we got to have a whole week off timetable to do this!

The title of my TOK essay was, 'Art is a lie that brings us closer to the truth. Discuss.' I found this really interesting and went on to look at similar questions when I studied Aesthetics as part of Philosophy at university.

The main part of CAS for me was the C. I did lots and lots of music. I played the flute, piano and saxophone, and studied the first two of these at the Guildhall School of Music and Drama in London.

What are you currently studying?
I am currently studying for a Master's degree in Economics. I also hold an MSc in Epistemology, Ethics and Mind, a PGCE in secondary Mathematics education, and a BA in Philosophy, Politics and Economics from the University of Oxford.

What was your favourite aspect(s)/specialism?
My favourite part of my undergraduate degree was political philosophy – arguing about seemingly abstract ideas that actually have a big impact on how we choose to live together in society.

In Economics, I really enjoy Behavioural Economics, looking at things like how we can employ certain policies to 'nudge' people into choosing actions that deliver the best outcomes, and Game Theory, which is all about how to make the best strategic decisions in given scenarios.

How did the IB prepare you for this?
Although I didn't do any of the subjects that I ended up studying at university for the IB, the IB curriculum enabled me to gain the analytical and critical thinking skills that I needed for my course. In addition, the extended essay was a really good way to get a feel for what writing university-style essays is like.

What are your plans for the future; what would you like to do after studying?
I would like to use my experience in the education sector as both a teacher in a secondary school and a tutor along with my Economics Master's in order to help craft better education policy.

What do you enjoy about tutoring?
I enjoy that lightbulb moment when you see a student understand something for the first time, and the way in which students grow in confidence across numerous tutorials.

What makes a successful tutor?

A successful tutor is someone who can break down complex ideas into small manageable parts, and then connect these parts back together again in a way the student understands. They need to be patient and encouraging.

What are your favourite aspects of the IB to teach, and why?

I like teaching Maths because it is a subject that is generally poorly taught in schools and students don't often get to appreciate the beauty of it and see how it all fits together conceptually.

What has been your greatest tutoring success?

Helping students get the grades that they need to go to university is always a highlight.

What tips do you have for current IB students?

Firstly, choose your options carefully – unlike A-levels you don't get a chance to drop any subjects after a year! And then, stay on top of your game in the first year and don't leave everything until the last term!

What are you best revision tips?

Test yourself constantly on what you are learning – **don't just revise passively**. The more exam questions you practice, the better you will do in the real thing.

Mix up different topics in your revision – don't do everything in huge blocks. Although it seems harder at the time, research has shown you remember more if you revise different topics together – remember, this is what the exam is going to look like!

What would do you differently next time?

Use past papers more to help with my revision, and redo papers having seen some feedback/looked at the answers – e.g. on a Maths paper not moving on with my revision

until I understood what I was struggling with 100%.

Luisa
IBDP score: 40
University: Biology (2018), University of Lisbon
Teaches: Biology, Maths, Spanish

Why did you choose to do the IB?

Doing the IB wasn't a very hard choice to make, having done the previous programmes (PYP and MYP), I always looked forward to choosing my subjects and finishing the IB successfully. The IB is not only a very complete program that allows you to push yourself in every single intellectual area, but it can also bring out the best in you (through CAS and by working as team) as a person.

What was the most challenging part of the IB?

What I found most challenging was keeping up with my extracurricular life, making sure I was spending enough time with friends and family even when I always felt I had something to do for school. Setting time away from studying is essential for so many reasons, not least to achieve your goals in school!

What are you currently studying?

I am currently in my last year of an undergraduate in Biology.

How did the IB prepare you for this?

The IB prepared me for my life at university because I got there already knowing how to manage my time, how to start a big project (through the EE), how to work in groups and make an organised presentation (through TOK and other subjects). A lot of my colleagues had never practiced these skills, so the time they spent worrying about those things, I spent working on the actual project and taking it to another level.

What tips do you have for current IB students?

Be organised from the start, listen carefully in

lessons and try to soak in as much as you can from your school time, that will make studying much simpler. Help your friends when they are stressed out – you will learn and maybe they will return the favour when you are in their position. Nobody does the IB by themselves, talk to your teachers about how you feel about their lessons or if you are struggling with something, they will most certainly help you out, ask for the cooperation of your family they like being involved!

How did you organise your revision?

The best thing I did was, when I finished each topic in each subject, I would make the final notes for that topic. That way when the final months before the exams came around I already had most of my notes done for every subject and I had time to review them carefully, and do all the past papers. Trust your notes, they were done when you still had a lot of time, and are probably much better than if you were to make new notes all over again!

What are you best revision tips?

Make studying fun an interactive by studying with friends. One at a time teach a full topic to the others, and the rest complete what he/she is saying by adding extra detail. You may disagree on somethings, but discussing them will really consolidate your knowledge, and you might find out that you were wrong about something crucial!

What would do you differently next time?

I would probably do my EE in a subject, one I was taking, it would have been a much smarter decision. But overall, I think the mistakes I made allowed me to grow and to do better next time. Don't worry if things don't go your way all the time, that is life, and being flexible and able to adapt is a great skill to have!

Javier
IBDP score: 41
University: The University of Edinburgh; Brown
Teaches: Chemistry, Biology, ESS

Why did you choose to do the IB?

I chose to do the IB because it's curriculum forms students that are actively engaged with their learning and encourages them to think critically. For me, it was very important to be challenged in the classrooms, rather than being forced to memorise concepts pointlessly.

Additionally, as a prospective Biology student, it was crucial for me to learn how to plan, conduct, and report a research project, which is central in all IB science subjects. Furthermore, from its design, the IB strives to promote intercultural understanding and environmental awareness, which are values very important to me.

What did you enjoy about the IB?

When I did the IB, I really enjoyed having the freedom to shape my high school education the way I wanted to, and at the same time, having the guidance of a very strong curriculum and well-prepared teachers. The IB syllabi allowed me to study in depth the subjects I wanted, and to focus my assignments on the topics I felt the most passionate about. For my Extended Essay, I further explored an idea that was especially interesting to me, and outside the classroom, I became very involved in CAS activities that caught my interest. Because of this, I was always fully engaged with all my classes and my extra-curricular activities, and I enjoyed all that I was doing.

What was the most challenging part of the IB?

The most challenging part of the IB for me was to efficiently manage my time to complete my assignments on a timely manner, revise difficult concepts throughout the semester, and participate in my CAS activities. The IB is a very rigorous curriculum that pushes students to excel in their studies. Nevertheless, time management is a skill that students must also work on developing in order to thrive in the IB. Additionally, studying for the final exams is a significant challenge. Revising two years' worth of subject content requires a great amount of planning in order to arrive to the exams feeling well prepared.

What did you do for your CAS and EE?

My **CAS** activities were central to my IB experience, as they complemented the academic formation I received in the classrooms. For my creation activity, I led the school's guitar club and performed in various events in the course of the two years; for my activity, I coordinated the tennis club; and for my service activity I helped teaching computer skills to adults in rural India, and taught English to orphan kids in the village nearby my school.

For my **Theory of Knowledge** Essay and Presentation, I discussed a Persian proverb that says that "doubt is the key to knowledge", arguing that moderate questioning and the seeking of answers are the bases of humanity's quest for knowledge. Nevertheless, excessive doubt can also lead to insecurity and lack of conclusions, which hinder the creation of new knowledge.

My Extended Essay explored the role of the Mexican government in the prevention and treatment of HIV/AIDS in Mexico.

Do you have any tips for current IB students?

My main advice for IB students is to always do work ahead and to never leave their work for the last minute. I strongly believe that the IB requires student to be constantly revising difficult concepts and to practice solving IB-style questions on a regular basis.

Studying for the IB must be a constant process rather than a single event that happens a few weeks before the final exams. The same idea applies for assignments, which require a lot of

dedication and hard work done over weeks or months, and not the night before it is due.

7. Appendices

7.1 Appendix 1: Full List of IB Diploma Subjects, 2018-19

Group 1

Language A: Literature. *Available currently in 55 languages, although not all are offered in both the May and November sessions. Others available on special request.*

Language A: Language & Literature. Currently available in 17 languages, again not all available in both sessions:
Arabic, Chinese, Dutch, English, French, German, Indonesian, Italian, Japanese, Korean, Modern Greek, Norwegian, Portuguese, Russian, Spanish, Swedish, Thai.

Language A: Literature & Performance. Available in English, Spanish, and French, although French and Spanish are by special request only.

Group 2

Language B: *23 languages offered*
Language ab initio: 12 languages offered
Classical languages: 2 languages offered

Language B languages: Arabic, Chinese- Cantonese, Chinese- Mandarin, Danish, Dutch, English, Finnish, French, German, Hebrew, Hindi, Indonesian, Italian, Japanese, Korean, Malay, Norwegian, Portuguese, Russian, Spanish, Swahili, Swedish, Tamil.
Language ab initio: Arabic, English, French, German, Indonesian, Italian, Japanese, Malay, Russian, Spanish, Swahili; *More languages available upon request & by special arrangements*

Classical Languages: Classical Greek, Latin

Group 3

Individuals & Societies: Business & Management, Economics, Environmental Systems & Societies (ESS) (also Gr4), Geography, Global Politics, History, Information Technology in a Global Society (ITGS), Philosophy, Psychology, Social & Cultural Anthropology, World Religions (SL only).

Group 4

Sciences: Biology; Computer Science; Chemistry; Design Technology; Environmental Systems & Societies (also Gr3); Physics; Sports, Exercise and Health Science.

Group 5

Mathematics: Mathematics Higher Level, Mathematics Standard Level, Mathematics Studies, Further Mathematics *(HL only)*

Group 6

Arts: Dance, Film, Music, Theatre, Visual Arts

7.2 Appendix 2: Contributors

The IB Guide is one of the most comprehensive resources for IB students, and is the result of years of expertise in support. The Guide was written by members of the EIB Education team (*), including our in-house team and some of the finest tutors we work with, to whom we extended our sincerest gratitude.

Beckett, Christopher*
Brookes, Charlotte*
Chang, Zhui Ning
Deden, Sophie

Fairbairn, Thomas
Flegontov, Daniil
Flores Kim, Javier
Gargan, Olga*
Gibson , Naomi*
Gonzalez, Michael
Hayes, Abigail*
Hills, Tiger*
Hoffmann, Timothy*
Hoffmann, Juliette*
Kwak, Jeehyun*
Lopez Matarranz, Andres*
Mandacaru, Luisa
Powell, Joshua*
Romeo, Salvatore*
Salim, Arzami*
Southworth Simons, Bella*
Symons, Anna
Wiberg, Ebba*
Willers, Thomas
Winters, Dara
Wood, Olivia
Yuen, Wei Hao*

Index

Notes

Notes

Notes

Notes

CPSIA information can be obtained
at www.ICGtesting.com
Printed in the USA
LVHW062130210620
658652LV00009B/942